BETTER THAN WELL?

BETTER THAN WELL?

The Most Important Question Facing Psychiatry

PAUL J. FITZGERALD, PH.D.

iUniverse LLC
Bloomington

iUniverse books may be ordered through booksellers or by contacting:

iUniverse LLC
1663 Liberty Drive
Bloomington, IN 47403
www.iuniverse.com
1-800-Authors (1-800-288-4677)

ISBN: 978-1-4917-1541-3 (sc)
ISBN: 978-1-4917-1542-0 (e)

Printed in the United States of America.

iUniverse rev. date: 12/03/2013

CONTENTS

ACKNOWLEDGEMENTS

This book is based on my years of research into the scientific and popular literature in the fields of neuroscience and psychiatry, and the conclusions I reached. It is not meant to substitute for the advice and care of a professional health care provider. My credentials for writing this book: I have a Ph.D. in neuroscience from Johns Hopkins University, and I performed postdoctoral behavioral neuroscience studies for nearly five years at the National Institutes of Health in the Washington, D.C. area. I am currently a behavioral neuroscientist in the Department of Psychology at Texas A&M University. I would like to thank my family and friends for their continuing support.

CHAPTER 1

Peter Kramer popularizes a concept

Is it possible, through use of existing psychiatric medications or talk therapy, to treat someone who has become slightly to severely mentally ill, and not only eliminate symptoms of his illness but also leave him "better than well"? This is a question with which eminent American psychiatrist, Peter Kramer, grappled in his landmark 1993 book, *Listening to Prozac*. Kramer concluded, based largely on responses of his own patients to the then relatively new antidepressant Prozac, that "better than well" may indeed be attainable in some persons. Not surprisingly, this is a controversial conclusion that has been met with a large degree of skepticism, including in a number of books that have since appeared.

Listening to Prozac included a number of fascinating case studies in which Kramer reported that not only could this drug improve depression or anxiety-related symptoms in his various patients, but also it seemed capable of transforming the very personality traits that are central to a person's identity. For example, Prozac seemed able to boost self-esteem in a manner in which psychotherapy may not have been as effective, or turn an inveterate wallflower into the life of the party.

Kramer opens the book with a case study of an architect he called Sam, who he describes as a charming and quirky guy of Austrian descent. Sam had become depressed after a reversal in his business fortunes and the death of his parents, and had consulted

Dr. Kramer. Sam had been somewhat obsessional as a child; for example, he had been inclined to spend hours rearranging his various collections of stamps and other items. Even though his obsessionality faded in adulthood, Kramer recommended a trial of Prozac, since this relatively new drug (at the time) was thought to be helpful in reducing compulsiveness, while also having antidepressant properties.

Soon after starting the drug, Sam declared that he was not only no longer depressed, but actually "better than well" (his very words). Sam felt more fully alive, less pessimistic. He was able to complete work-related projects much more efficiently, and could present his work in front of groups without using any notes. His concentration was better and his memory sharper. And strangely enough, Sam also lost all interest in his former hobby of watching pornographic videos. On this last point, Sam felt Prozac had in some ways freed him of an addiction. Overall, Sam found his "personality transformation" on this drug both favorable and somewhat disconcerting.

Another one of Kramer's patients, a woman he called Tess, also showed a remarkable response to Prozac. Tess, the daughter of an alcoholic father, grew up in a public-housing project and was sexually abused in childhood. In spite of this harsh upbringing, Tess was able to stay in school and help direct her younger siblings into stable jobs and marriages. She herself got married at seventeen to an older man, who was both abusive and an alcoholic, and this marriage eventually collapsed. Afterward, she found herself in a string of affairs with abusive married men. In spite of her unhappy personal life, Tess was having a successful career in the business world, helping turn around struggling companies. However, after suffering the demoralization of having another one of her affairs end, she slipped into a state of clinical depression, which psychotherapy alone was not able to reverse.

Upon meeting Tess after consulting with her psychotherapist, Dr. Kramer was surprised to find the she was both charming and a pleasure to be with, even when depressed; the scars were well-hidden, as he put it. After Tess only showed a weak response to an older antidepressant (imipramine), Kramer prescribed Prozac. Two weeks later, Tess declared that she felt rested, energized, and hopeful, for the first time in ages. She laughed more often, and her laughter was no longer restrained, but lively and even teasing. Her social life was altered radically almost overnight, as now she had more dates with men than she could handle, and could scarcely believe she had once entered into such unhealthy relationships with married men. Tess's circle of friends also changed, partly because some may only have been able to relate with her while she was depressed. Her professional life also became more rewarding, as she felt firmer and less conciliatory when negotiating with union leaders; she was more confident. Tess now indeed felt that she had been depressed her whole life, and that Prozac had suddenly freed her from this great burden.

A third patient of Kramer's, who he called Julia, also provides an interesting case study on the effects of Prozac. Julia had contacted Dr. Kramer because she thought she resembled a patient Kramer had written about in a magazine article who had responded well to Prozac. Julia was not depressed, but was frazzled at work and especially in her family life, where she was highly compulsive and demanded extraordinary orderliness with everything. She did not exhibit a full-blown case of obsessive-compulsive disorder (OCD), but she did show a great deal of perfectionism in her dealings with her husband and children, and was continually angry with them. Although Dr. Kramer did not want to dispense a "mother's little helper" medication, he was willing to test whether Prozac would improve Julia's quality of life and prescribed the drug.

Within the first week on drug, she felt energized and got along with her children and husband much better; she said she "could not have imagined this", meaning that she didn't think her response was a placebo effect. Julia could tolerate messiness much more easily now. There were ups and downs in the weeks that followed, and Dr. Kramer gradually increased the dose of Prozac, since OCD often responds best to high doses of drugs like Prozac and Julia may have had a milder version of a full-blown case. And she steadily improved. She quit her part-time job and started a much

3

more stressful one, doing hospital shift-work, and eventually settled on pediatric nursing that required much tolerance of unpredictable children. Julia felt her life and outlook had been transformed by Prozac.

About six months into this pharmacological experiment, Dr. Kramer thought they should try lowering the dose of the drug, as the long-term effects of such a medication are not well understood. Two weeks later, Julia told him that she was back to square one, fighting with her family members and hating her job. She told Kramer she "was a witch again". They raised the dose again and she soon had a similar favorable response as before.

Kramer ends this case report on Julia by reminding the reader that Julia had originally contacted him because of a magazine article he had written about another patient of his. That patient was Tess! Kramer goes on to speculate that the two women may indeed have had something biologically in common, and I would speculate that it may be compulsiveness.

*   *   *

These are certainly provocative observations made by Kramer (and his patients), and not surprisingly he has been attacked, either directly or indirectly, in a number of subsequent books, such as *Talking Back to Prozac, Let them Eat Prozac, Artificial Happiness,* and *Manufacturing Depression.* These authors and other critics of his book seem to largely address the following three possibly related points: 1) they suggest Kramer is irresponsibly advocating widespread use of Prozac and related drugs, 2) they don't believe Prozac can transform personality traits (that is, make people "different from well"), 3) nor do they believe people can be rendered "better than well" by Prozac. Regarding point one: the argument could be made that Kramer is actually suggesting that Prozac and related drugs should *not* be put into widespread use, particularly when we don't fully understand the drug's effects on the individual, as well as on society as a whole. He was concerned with (and remains so, to my knowledge) the societal, philosophical, and moral ramifications of making such a drug available to the public on a broad scale. Instead of directly promoting its use, he was merely observing that this drug, in some cases at least, can produce remarkably positive effects, while also producing alterations in personality. Regarding points two and three: while a psychiatrist's impression of the transformative properties of an antidepressant drug may be difficult to verify, there is now a large scientific literature, consisting both of animal and human studies, indicating that Prozac and related drugs alter a number of aspects of behavior and brain function itself, and some of these alterations may indeed be related to what we call "personality".

Part of the backlash against *Listening to Prozac*, in books such as *Let them Eat Prozac*, is against "Big Pharma" itself, which comprises the enormous multinational corporations that dominate the landscape of today's pharmaceutical industry. One of these large companies is Eli Lilly, the creator of Prozac and other blockbuster psychiatric drugs, including Zyprexa and Cymbalta. Marcia Angell, former Editor of the New England Journal of Medicine and author of *The Truth About the Drug Companies*, is one of the outspoken opponents of this industry. She suggests that these companies are largely marketing machines, doing little to bring original drugs to market that would benefit the field of medicine. While I believe she is correct that there is a great deal of emphasis on "pushing pills" to people in the dog-eat-dog climate of today's pharmaceutical industry, these companies still serve a critically important function of absorbing the tremendous cost and financial risk of bringing new drugs to market. And another underappreciated function of these companies is that they tend to very reliably supply their drugs to people throughout the world.

It is certainly true that the pharmaceutical industry has changed a great deal since the 1950s and 1960s, when many of today's psychiatric drugs were first being synthesized, before the days of Prozac (which was brought to market in 1987). To my knowledge, pharmaceutical companies were not largely vilified by the public in the mid-twentieth century, which was an era of much lower industry-wide competition, when it was easier to invent drugs with unprecedented mechanisms of action because a lot less had already been discovered. These companies probably began to be vilified in recent decades, perhaps particularly in the United States, when they orchestrated large-scale marketing efforts, directly toward the general public and toward doctors who prescribe their drugs.

Backlash regarding the value of the pharmaceutical industry in general, and antidepressants in particular, has recently culminated in biomedical researcher Irving Kirsch suggesting, in various scientific publications as well as in the book *The Emperor's New Drugs*, that antidepressants actually do next to nothing beneficial for people who take them. I will discuss this idea more in the next chapter, but let me state here that I agree with Kirsch that, *in the manner in which antidepressants are currently used*, they have no or very little therapeutic value for most people who use them. The reason for this ineffectiveness may be that these drugs are not being used properly in the vast majority of cases, and later in the book I will present ideas on how to use them, and other psychiatric drugs, more effectively. The basic idea is that the correct drug, or pair of drugs, is typically not being given to the person at the right dose for a sufficient amount of time.

In spite of these criticisms of antidepressants in general and *Listening to Prozac* in particular, a premise of this book is that Peter Kramer has identified a critically important, and yet to be fully addressed, issue for the field of psychiatry. I am suggesting that verifying the existence of "better than well" is the most important question facing psychiatry. One could argue that a more important question than "better than well" is simply how to treat the overtly mentally ill in a more effective manner, how to render them "normal" or simply "well"? However, I will suggest that the key to making the slightly to severely mentally ill "well" may actually lie in implementing better than well treatment in them. After all, a very large fraction of mentally ill persons are still not able to function after receiving conventional drug and talk therapy treatments, so perhaps trying to render them better than well with revised treatment methods may, for a variety of reasons, produce higher quality of life and enable them to function again (or perhaps for the first time). For example, psychiatric drugs often produce numerous, significant side effects, and implementing the positive qualities of better than well treatment may compensate for these negative aspects of drug treatment. If the effect of better than well is large enough, perhaps even severely afflicted persons could reach a level of health and contentment where they are no longer considered sick at all.

I will argue in this book that "better than well" does indeed exist. In assessing the existing evidence, largely from the scientific literature published in the last several decades, the more clearly unresolved issue may be to identify what fraction of the population could be rendered better than well, and to what degree, with existing or yet to be created drugs. However, a perhaps less controversial claim at this point may support another catchy phrase, "different from well". This means psychiatric drugs or talk therapy may change a person's mental characteristics and behavioral patterns, rendering her different from how she used to be, although not necessarily making her "better off". The rest of this book examines these issues in greater detail, including analysis of cutting edge neuroscience research, while suggesting ways to treat various mental illnesses more effectively with existing psychiatric drugs, and assessing how large-scale treatment of mild to severe mental illness, or even "normal" individuals, may eventually affect society.

CHAPTER 2

Zooming in on better than well

This chapter will focus on how better than well may be defined, while also elaborating upon some of its implications and providing more details on the concept. In the first chapter, I suggested that one definition of better than well involves rendering people who become mentally ill better than they were before they became sick. Expansion of this definition could include rendering people who have been significantly mentally ill (or perhaps just slightly sick, or even "normal") *their whole lives*, better than they have ever been. This expanded definition touches upon a key point that Peter Kramer addressed in his 1997 Afterword to *Listening to Prozac*: whether Prozac and other so-called SSRIs affect "normals". (Note: the term "SSRIs" stands for selective serotonin reuptake inhibitors; these are a family of related antidepressant drugs that selectively boost the neurotransmitter serotonin and include Zoloft, Paxil, Celexa, Lexapro, and Luvox.) Kramer stated that this "is a question I avoided answering in the book. There is still no large-scale, definitive research on that topic, although leading scientists have proposed the critical studies that would settle the matter. The small studies that have come to my attention all point in one direction: these medications do have the power to affect 'normals'—people without any psychiatric diagnosis."

A number of scientific studies published since 1997 have supported Kramer's assertion. For example, a placebo controlled study (which is a study where some people receive drug and others merely receive an inactive pill, and the persons aren't aware of which treatment they were given) in which the SSRI Lexapro was given to healthy persons found that it altered moral judgments. These persons were presented with hypothetical moral dilemmas, where they were asked, for example, if they would allow an innocent person to be killed if it would save five other lives? Enhancing serotonin with Lexapro made the people in the study more likely to judge harmful actions as forbidden, but only for emotionally salient hypothetical harms. Another placebo controlled study of Lexapro in healthy persons examined the drug's effect on social interaction with a roommate in an apartment over several weeks, as well as subsequent interaction with a stranger. On drug, the persons were rated as less submissive by their roommates, showed a dominant pattern of eye contact and were more cooperative in interacting with the stranger in a role playing game. A third placebo controlled study of Lexapro, in healthy females, where drug was given transiently in an intravenous manner, found that Lexapro selectively enhanced recognition of facial expressions of fear and happiness presented on a video monitor, without affecting recognition of other emotions. In this short-term study, Lexapro did not affect measures of mood. These studies support Kramer's claim that serotonergic antidepressants have behavioral effects in "normal" persons. (Note: many studies of SSRIs use Lexapro because it is considered the drug from this class that is most selective for serotonin, as opposed to affecting other chemical targets and receptors in the brain.)

*   *   *

A central point in *Listening to Prozac*, which is intertwined with the concept of better than well, is the idea that Prozac and related drugs can, most likely through serotonergic mechanisms, transform personality. The above three studies, particularly the first two, suggest that these drugs may indeed alter personality traits in healthy persons. SSRIs may also alter personality traits in persons with diagnosed mental illness, which may to some degree be independent of their particular illness. A study of Paxil in persons with major depression or obsessive-compulsive disorder found that this drug, while not showing differences in effect between these two groups, reduced the trait of "harm avoidance" (that is, avoiding bad things) in drug responders more so than in non-responders, and on the whole tended to increase social dominance and decrease hostility in social situations in those treated with drug. An intriguing study of persons with major depression measured the effects of Zoloft on psychopathic personality traits. Independent of its effects on depression, Zoloft increased adaptive traits traditionally observed in psychopathic individuals, including social charm and interpersonal and physical boldness. On the other hand Zoloft reduced maladaptive traits associated with psychopathy, including impulsivity (that is, acting on a whim without thinking things through). This study may suggest that a psychopath treated with an SSRI would still be a psychopath, albeit with altered behavioral characteristics.

These studies and others do not necessarily indicate that personality alterations on SSRIs can leave a person better than well, but it seems likely that they can at least render her "different from well." In other words, an individual can be transformed by these drugs, although whether she really is better off is a matter of debate. One could certainly argue, for example, that being more assertive socially is a good thing, but such behavior may also have negative consequences in particular circumstances. Different from well is the focus of a later chapter in this book, but it is an important concept to consider throughout as we evaluate merits of the better than well theory. Related to the concept of different from well is that of potentially "worse than well" effects of SSRIs and other psychiatric drugs, where these negative outcomes may not be limited to standard side effects of the drugs. What I mean is that, for example, an SSRI may indeed raise serotonin in a given person and thereby, perhaps paradoxically, produce *negative* effects on personality, mood, or other characteristics. In this scenario, perhaps the person had genetically elevated serotonin signaling to begin with, so raising the level further has negative consequences.

Another issue in assessing the concept of better than well is whether talk therapy, which is more formally referred to as "psychotherapy", alone can render a person better off? It very well may have this ability, a statement with which Kramer might agree. But as with psychiatric drugs, talk therapy may result in a worse than well outcome in some cases.

Regarding personality transformation produced by drugs or talk therapy: I have suggested in my previous book, *Adjust Your Brain*, that producing better than well in a given person may give her less of a "specialized" personality and render her more so a "generalist", in that she becomes capable of a broader range of constructive behaviors. Perhaps the brain basis of this putative effect is that brain circuits that were previously "shut off" by dysthmia (which is chronic, low grade depression) or other mild mental illness, become functional for the first time. It is an open question as to whether this generalist concept is indeed correct. Perhaps existing drugs such as Prozac produce only subtle changes in personality, leaving the "self" largely intact, while potentially producing large increases in contentment or quality of life, especially in persons with severe mental illness. To some degree, we may all have stereotyped, specialized personalities (absentminded professor, eccentric billionaire, corporate alpha male or female, etc) that are resistant to pharmacological intervention. If so, perhaps that's a good thing, both for ourselves and for society in general.

* * *

Trying to characterize better than well in detail, in terms of its exact effects on personality and behavior, is not easily accomplished, partly because the effects of SSRIs and related psychiatric drugs on the brain are not fully known. Moreover, the brain systems these drugs act upon, including serotonin and related neurotransmitters such as norepinephrine, dopamine, and acetylcholine, are not completely understood. If they were, we might close down the shop of neuroscience, but this probably won't be happening anytime soon, if ever.

Aside from the vague statement that people may be rendered "better off" by psychiatric drugs such as SSRIs, what precisely is meant by this potentially profound statement? I'm afraid there's no simple answer to this question. Defining what exactly better than well *does* to people may be a little like the blind men and the elephant parable, where depending on which part of the elephant one happens to grasp, you get a different answer, where it's difficult to see the big picture. For example, better than well may be related to improvement in mood, but what exactly does this entail, in terms of the subjective experience, in a given person? Is mood improvement the same for different individuals? Similar arguments can be made about improvement in cognition, positive emotion, anxiety level, sensory responsiveness, self-esteem, confidence, or ability to experience pleasure, with SSRIs and related drugs. Effects on additional traits also remain to be determined.

Overall, what I'm suggesting is that we probably haven't identified all of the characteristics through which these drugs may produce better than well outcomes, and for the characteristics we have identified, the effects may be experienced differently by various individuals, making those putative changes difficult to define. In other words, the manifestation of better than well may be highly subjective and dependent upon the individual. But this doesn't mean the concept doesn't exist, or that there aren't similar changes across individuals produced by a given psychiatric drug or class of drugs. Indeed, the scientific studies mentioned thus far suggest that SSRIs can produce similar effects across individuals, such as increasing assertiveness or, in Peter Kramer's clients, decreasing compulsiveness. Perhaps one can draw an analogy between better than well and the concept of quantum mechanics in theoretical physics: they are unconventional topics that are difficult to believe, partly because they are counterintuitive and difficult to grasp.

Is better than well actually hypomania (that is, mild mania) or an "amphetaminelike high" produced by SSRIs or related drugs?

Peter Kramer touches upon this idea in *Listening to Prozac* and concludes that this is not the case. I agree: while antidepressants can certainly induce hypomania or outright mania in the small proportion of individuals who suffer from bipolar disorder, many of the changes produced by Prozac and related drugs, such as decreased aggressiveness or diminished impulsivity, do not resemble symptoms of hypomania or mania.

*   *   *

Does better than well merely produce a "cosmetic" change in the individual, without fundamentally changing her subjective experience of the world? Peter Kramer, in coining the term "cosmetic psychopharmacology", would probably assert that SSRIs do both: they alter the nature of the individual while also affecting how she interacts with others in the world. This is a critical point. If these drugs only affect social interaction, without fundamentally altering how the person views herself or experiences life aside from through others, then their effect on a person is quite superficial and, I feel, relatively inconsequential in terms of quality of life for that person, especially after she adapts to her potentially enhanced social skills after some time. I would argue that the most important effects of these drugs are far more than "skin deep", with potentially profound effects on mood and self-worth for example, and that such effects are far more fundamental than simply affecting social interaction.

Lending credence to the psychiatric concept of better than well, it seems that correction of non-brain based functions can also render a person "better off." Better than well for the body is the subject of a later chapter, but let me provide an example now. If someone has a high, largely genetically determined level of cholesterol, that he has had practically all his life, and he takes a statin drug that lowers the level to within the normal range (without producing any significant side effects), is he better than well? I'd say he is. A similar case can be made for high blood pressure or asthma treatment with pharmaceutical agents. In this later chapter, I describe a theory that I've put forth in a variety of scientific publications that suggests norepinephrine, which is a neurotransmitter that is related to serotonin, plays a causative role in a wide variety of non-brain based disorders, including diabetes, glaucoma, lupus, and some types of cancer.

Regarding pharmaceutical treatment of the mentally ill: is rendering people better than well with an antidepressant such as Prozac just limited to ameliorating depression, or does it treat a variety of psychiatric disorders, or even neurological disorders as well? Kramer suggests that Prozac (and by inference, serotonin) affects a broad spectrum of brain functions, including affecting a wide range of personality traits, and this may translate into broad effectiveness in brain-based disorders. This sentiment is echoed by psychiatrist Michael Norden in his book, *Beyond Prozac*. Psychiatry and neurology have traditionally been considered separate medical fields, but this distinction may be arbitrary and is blurred by drugs such as Prozac. One could argue that neurology to some degree deals with irreversible or deteriorating conditions such as Alzheimer's disease, Parkinson's disease, and epilepsy, whereas psychiatry does not. But psychiatric conditions such as schizophrenia may be to some degree irreversible (and deteriorating) and neurological disorders may eventually prove to be reversible with new treatment methods, pharmaceutical and otherwise.

One could also argue that neurology deals with "organic" brain disorders, whereas psychiatry deals with disorders of the "mind". This is most likely an outmoded view as well, as scientists are elucidating the biological, brain-based component of psychiatric disorders as well. This, however, does not rule out a non-brain-based component to mental functioning, related to the ideas of philosophers such as Rene Descartes on the topic of "dualism". Many scientists and doctors today would probably laugh at the possibility that all of mental functioning is not produced directly by properties of the brain alone. But this is an issue that, in my opinion, will probably never be fully resolved by empirical studies of the brain, regardless of one's beliefs on spirituality in general or institutionalized religion in particular.

So better than well may unify psychiatry and neurology, partly through the overlapping effectiveness of Prozac and related drugs on psychiatric and neurological disorders, and partly due to co-existence of these disorders in the same person (that is, "comorbidity" of these disorders).

*   *   *

How will we know if someone has been rendered better than well by a pharmaceutical agent? And how will we know beforehand if a given person, whether mentally ill or essentially "normal", has the potential of being rendered better than well by existing drugs? The way other people are, whether content, dissatisfied, happy, sad, or none of the above, lies to some degree in the eye of the beholder, including as revealed through social interaction. While there are objective data on human nature from scientific studies, trying to understand other people is to some degree inherently subjective, influenced by one's own nature. This argument may apply to all of the inquisitive folks who throughout history have examined and written about human nature. The list includes Hippocrates, Freud, Jung, Kraepelin, and many others. Like Peter Kramer wrote of Freud, we tend to take elements of our own experiences and turn them into a universal. This may well lead us to incorrect inferences if people actually tend to be very different from one another, including in how they experience the world. It may indeed "take all types to make the world go 'round", and in my opinion different individuals, who often behave very differently from one another, do so because they are fundamentally and vastly different from the inside out.

One of the biggest obstacles we face in testing the better than well hypothesis, or even the different from well one, is simply how to verify that someone's mental state and/or behavior has been altered by a drug or talk therapy. We can ask her questions that probe her mental state, but questioning may only produce a limited, murky picture of the internal state. Another option is to use brain scans, such as functional magnetic resonance imaging (fMRI) and positron emission tomography (PET), to measure changes in neural activity. A third possibility is to measure behavior, essentially treating the brain as a "black box", as in the behaviorists from the mid-twentieth century such as B.F. Skinner. Many aspects of behavior, such as sweating or eye blinking, can be objectively measured, but they do not necessarily provide an accurate or objective measure of psychological state.

Regarding the subjective effects of antidepressants, how is the experience of better than well, or different from well, described by people who have taken these drugs, in addition to the comments of Kramer's patients described earlier? Elizabeth Wurtzel, in her famous memoir *Prozac Nation*, wrote the Prozac didn't make her happy, just not sad. Lauren Slater, in her beautifully written memoir *Prozac Diary*, suggested that Prozac is "Zen medicine" in helping relieve her symptoms of obsessive-compulsive disorder. Stephen Braun, author of *The Science of Happiness*, a book that did not receive nearly as much attention as it deserved, observed that the antidepressant Wellbutrin heightened his interest in the opposite sex, and also decreased his desire to consume drinks that contain caffeine or alcohol.

*   *   *

The issue of better than well raises a fundamental question about the functioning of the brain: is it optimized for performance in the vast majority of individuals, or is it "kluge"? Whether you believe in evolution, intelligent design, or both (as is the case for Francis Collins, eminent geneticist and current head of the National Institutes of Health), it is unclear whether the brain, for most persons, runs like a new Ferrari or is instead leaking oil and missing a few hubcaps. The researchers David Linden and Gary Marcus have argued, in their respective books *The Accidental Mind* and *Kluge*, that evolution has rendered the brain sloppily arranged, where it would not be surprising to find suboptimal performance, including mental illness.

One can make similar arguments about other aspects of the body. Taking the eye as an example, the layers of cells in the retina appear to be arranged in an illogical fashion, with the light sensing rods and cones buried beneath the other layers of cells, instead of being in the outer layer to better sense light. A counterpoint to this "kluge" example is the eye is nonetheless so sensitive we can detect a single photon of light. One point that is established about human vision is that many people require eyeglasses or contact lenses to see properly, so this aspect of eye functioning is definitely imperfect in a large fraction of the population. Whether an analogous situation exists for mild to severe mental illness, whereby drugs such as Prozac can correct the brain equivalent of "blurry vision", as Stephen Braun and I have independently argued in our previous books, remains to be determined.

CHAPTER 3

The chemicals between us

This chapter shifts gears and provides an introduction to the brain chemistry that is involved in mental illness, with an emphasis on neurotransmitter systems. This information is critical to understanding how we may render persons better than well with existing pharmaceutical agents. Neurotransmitters, which are molecules that brain cells use to communicate with one another, may form a critical part of the story in mental illness, but they are not the whole story. For example, they interact with a number of key molecular pathways within cells that are also critical for mental health. The neurotransmitters serotonin, norepinephrine, and dopamine—the so-called "biogenic amines", a name that is related to their molecular structure—have probably received the most attention in public discussions of mental illness. I will discuss these three molecules in this chapter, while also providing information on some less frequently discussed neurotransmitters— acetylcholine, GABA, glutamate, and a few others. I will also touch upon some of the molecular pathways inside brain cells with which these neurotransmitters interact. In the next chapter, I will put this information into action, by discussing how abnormalities in these brain signaling mechanisms may produce mental illness.

Here are a few basic principles of neurotransmitter systems. Brain cells called neurons typically are not directly connected with one another, and instead communicate by sending molecules called neurotransmitters across small gaps called synapses. Often, one neuron (called the presynaptic cell) releases the neurotransmitter, which floats across the synapse and attaches to specialized molecules called receptors on the outside of the receiving neuron (which is called the postsynaptic cell). A particular type of neurotransmitter attaches to particular types of postsynaptic receptors, in a lock and key fashion. Attaching of the neurotransmitter to the postsynaptic cell's receptors produces one of two basic types of responses in that cell, depending on the type of receptor: 1) so-called ionotropic receptors allow charged particles (that is, ions) to flow into or out of the cell through a pore in the receptor, thereby affecting the electrical excitability of the cell; 2) so-called metabotropic receptors influence molecular pathways inside the cell, which can have numerous consequences. Ionotropic receptors tend to have faster effects on the neuron than metabotropic receptors. Nearly all of the known serotonin, norepinephrine, and dopamine receptors are metabotropic, which may suggest that at least some of the effects of these three neurotransmitters on brain function are rather steady and act slowly.

In addition to the receptors on the postsynaptic cell, in many cases the presynaptic neuron also has receptors on its outside surface for the neurotransmitter it is releasing. These so-called presynaptic receptors, also known as autoreceptors, typically regulate the release of the neurotransmitter, such that when a lot has been released into the synapse, the autoreceptors can sense this and shut off further release. In addition to autoreceptors regulating release, the brain has three basic ways of shutting off neurotransmitter signaling once these molecules have been released into a synapse: 1) diffusion—which simply means the molecules float away, 2) reuptake—which means the transmitter is moved back into the presynaptic neuron through specialized molecular "pumps", 3) inactivation—which entails breaking down the transmitter into inactive molecules through the workings of molecules called enzymes that can be present in the synapse or inside the presynaptic neuron. The neurotransmitter acetylcholine is different from many other transmitters in that it does not have reuptake pumps (except for its broken down molecule), and relies more so on inactivation by an enzyme called acetylcholinesterase to terminate its signaling. Hence, drugs called cholinesterase inhibitors, which are used to treat Alzheimer's disease, boost the synaptic level of acetylcholine by weakening the activity of the cholinesterase enzyme.

Each of the neurotransmitters mentioned above has more than one type of receptor to which it can attach. These are called receptor "subtypes", and they differ from one another in molecular structure. For serotonin, seven basic subtypes of receptors, called 5-HT_1 through 5-HT_7 (where "5-HT" is an abbreviation for serotonin's formal name, 5-hydroxytryptamine), have been identified by scientists. To complicate matters further for understanding the serotonin signaling system, there are subtypes within the subtypes. This tends to be the case for the other neurotransmitter systems as well. Norepinephrine has five basic subtypes of receptors (α_1, α_2, β_1, β_2, β_3); the first two are called "alpha" receptors, and the last three "beta" receptors. You may well have heard the terms "alpha blocker" or "beta blocker", which refer to pharmaceutical drugs that block activation of these receptors and are often used to treat heart-related ailments, since these receptors are not only in the brain but also in the heart and other organs of the body. Dopamine has five basic subtypes of receptors as well, D_1 through D_5, where D_1 and D_5 are closely related structurally and functionally, and the other three (D_2, D_3, D_4) form another distinct group. Acetylcholine receptors comprise two basic subtypes: nicotinic and muscarinic, with multiple varieties within each subtype. Nicotinic receptors are ionotropic, and muscarinic receptors are metabotropic. Nicotine, which is the principal active ingredient in tobacco products, attaches to and activates nicotinic receptors, which could be related to the anxiety-reducing effect of smoking cigarettes.

GABA, which is the brain's principal "inhibitory" neurotransmitter in that it tends to quell neural activity, has two major subtypes of receptors, called $GABA_A$ and $GABA_B$. $GABA_A$

receptors are ionotropic and allow negatively charged chloride ions to flow into the cell, thereby reducing excitability. $GABA_B$ receptors are metabotropic and can initiate signaling pathways inside the cell that, like $GABA_A$ receptors, reduce excitability. There are multiple varieties of both $GABA_A$ and $GABA_B$ receptors.

Glutamate, the brain's principal "excitatory" neurotransmitter, has a complex array of receptor subtypes: three subtypes of ionotropic receptors (called AMPA, kainate, and NMDA receptors), as well as multiple varieties of metabotropic receptors. Of these various subtypes, AMPA and NMDA receptors are strongly associated with learning and memory functions in a wide range of brain circuits. Two drugs that are frequently abused, ketamine ("Special K") and PCP ("angel dust"), block the activity of NMDA receptors and produce distortions in perception of reality.

Another class of neurotransmitter molecules has received less attention than those described above: the so-called peptide transmitters, which are small proteins. When we think of proteins, we typically associate them with nutrition, building strong bones and the like. But peptide transmitters help neurons communicate, similarly to their more well-known siblings that are listed above. One example is neuropeptide y, which can be released from cells along with other neurotransmitters such as norepinephrine. There are five subtypes of neuropeptide y receptors, called Y_1 through Y_5.

In the last decade or so, another class of neurotransmitters has come into prominence in scientific circles, the so-called endocannabinoids. As their name suggests, these molecules interact with the same receptor class that the street drug marijuana (also known as cannabis) acts upon to produce its "high". The surprising finding here is that the body produces its own marijuana-related molecules, called endocannabinoids, which activate the same receptors that THC, the principal active ingredient in marijuana, acts upon. The two known subtypes of endocannabinoid receptors are called CB_1 and CB_2, and both are metabotropic, where CB_1 is the principal brain endocannabinoid receptor. Elucidating the function of endocannabinoids and their receptors is, along with all other neurotransmitter systems, an area of active research. It is already clear that these molecules have a diverse array of functions, including appetite regulation and learning and memory functions, which are unrelated to simply making us "high".

*   *   *

Now that we've discussed the receptors for many of the prominent neurotransmitter systems, what about the molecular pathways inside of neurons which many of these receptors modulate? One of the principal pathways involves a molecule called cyclic AMP, or cAMP for short. Some of the receptors described above, such as the D_1 dopamine receptor, activate production of cAMP, whereas other receptors, such as D_2, reduce its production. Hence, different receptor subtypes within a neurotransmitter system, such as dopamine, may have opposing functions. An interesting point about cAMP is that we can trace its function all the way to regulation of the cell's DNA, which is where the genetic information of the cell is stored. By modulating a cascade of molecular signaling pathways, where one molecule interacts with the next and so forth, cAMP can regulate the so-called transcription of genes, whereby certain genes are turned on and others are turned off. Such gene regulation can have dramatic effects on the cell's signaling properties, and even affect whether the cell dies, holds steady, or makes copies of itself. Gene regulation is related to the phenomenon of "neurogenesis", which comprises birth of new neurons in animals and humans, and gene regulation may also be related to cancer both in the brain and in other organs of the body.

Since I've now outlined the major receptor subtypes for the above neurotransmitter systems, what does this information tell us about the complexity and relative importance of each system? One simple interpretation is that the greater the number of receptor subtypes, the more complex the transmitter system. This reasoning may suggest that glutamate is the most complex neurotransmitter system, a conclusion that may indeed be correct. A potentially related issue is whether the complexity of the receptor subtype array for a given transmitter system indicates the relative importance of that system. After all, a given transmitter system does not exist in a void, and the ones described above interact in multiple ways within the brain, including that their different receptors are often located on the same neurons. So which ones are the generals and which are the foot soldiers, if there indeed is a hierarchical relationship across neurotransmitter systems (or within systems in terms of opposition between receptor subtypes)? We might be tempted to conclude that the complex glutamate system is also the most important transmitter system—a general and not a foot soldier—but I don't think this is the case, even though glutamate is of critical importance to brain signaling. Instead, I think some of the so-called modulatory neurotransmitters—serotonin, norepinephrine, dopamine, acetylcholine—are actually the "bosses", and glutamate and GABA are their "employees". Part of the reason I've reached this conclusion is the existence of widely-ranging effects of drugs that act on the modulatory transmitters, where these signaling molecules produce a great diversity of effects while interacting with circuits throughout the brain, a molecular endpoint of which may be alteration of glutamate and GABA signaling. Lending credence to the analogy of generals and foot soldiers for neurotransmitter systems: different brain areas, such as the many that process visual information, appear to have a hierarchical relationship with one another.

Related to these points, there are three ways I think of the relationship between receptor subtypes within a transmitter system, as well as the relationship between different transmitter systems: alignment, opposition, and independence. Alignment means that two receptor subtypes, or two transmitter systems, produce similar or identical effects on a given brain function, such as a particular aspect of memory. Opposition means that the two subtypes, or the two whole transmitter systems, counteract one another for the given function. Independence means that the given subtypes or transmitter systems have unrelated effects on the given function or different functions. There may be examples of alignment, opposition, or independence within and across all of the above transmitter systems, and this is an area of active research.

Comparison of two prominent neurotransmitter systems involved in mental health, serotonin and norepinephrine, may provide examples of functional alignment, opposition, and independence. Regarding alignment, both of these transmitters have a complex relationship with the operational properties of an important brain region called the prefrontal cortex, which is located toward the front of the brain as the name implies. Pharmaceutical drugs that enhance either serotonin or norepinephrine signaling can reduce impulsivity (which means acting on a whim without thinking things through), both in animal models and in humans, an effect that may be mediated by interaction with the prefrontal cortex. In contrast, a recent scientific paper I wrote suggests that serotonin and norepinephrine may be opposed to one another in terms of "lateralized" functions of the brain, with serotonin tending to activate the right side of the brain and norepinephrine the left. Regarding potential independence of function between these two transmitters: in the 1980s, eminent psychiatric researcher C. Robert Cloninger suggested that serotonin modulates a behavioral effect called "harm avoidance" that was mentioned above, whereas norepinephrine modulates "reward dependence". To greatly simplify Cloninger's ideas, harm avoidance is related to avoiding bad things, whereas reward dependence is related to seeking good things. Thus, the complex relationship between serotonin and norepinephrine may provide examples of functional alignment, opposition, and independence.

Another way I think serotonin and norepinephrine may show functional opposition is by serotonin largely being an inhibitory transmitter, whereas norepinephrine may be largely excitatory. This means by interacting with its receptors, serotonin largely turns off brain electrical activity, whereas norepinephrine turns it on. I have published a scientific paper suggesting that epilepsy, which typically involves elevated brain electrical activity, may be partially caused by increased norepinephrine signaling (although, paradoxically, *decreased* norepinephrine signaling is also implicated in epilepsy). If serotonin is largely inhibitory and norepinephrine largely excitatory, there may still be functional opposition in this regard *within* their groups of receptors, but the overall effect of serotonin would be to suppress brain activity and norepinephrine to enhance it, at least for most circuits and functions.

A more general theory is that the brain has a family of inhibitory transmitters, as well as a family of excitatory ones. Inhibitory ones may include (but not be limited to) serotonin, GABA, dopamine, and acetylcholine. Excitatory ones may include (but not be limited to) norepinephrine, glutamate, neuropeptide y, and the "stress hormone" cortisol. One line of information I've used to make this classification is based on the actions of the receptors of these transmitters, including how they interact with cAMP signaling: receptors that increase this signaling may be excitatory and those that decrease it may be inhibitory. A more complex theory is that some, if not all, transmitters straddle the divide between being exclusively inhibitory or solely excitatory; dopamine may be an example of such a "hybrid" transmitter system.

Another aspect of neurotransmitter functioning, which has been studied in vivid detail by Anthony Grace and his colleagues at the University of Pittsburgh, is so-called tonic or phasic release. Grace has focused on dopamine and has shown that it can be released in a rather slow and steady manner (that is, tonically), or instead in a fast and short-lasting way (that is, phasically). While understanding phasic release is certainly of high importance in understanding how these transmitter systems work, tonic release may be of higher importance to understanding how transmitter systems produce long-lasting effects associated with mental health and illness, such as our mood. In describing the overall, rather steady effect of a transmitter system on our mental health, I use the term "strength" to signify the tonic synaptic level of the transmitter throughout the brain, as well as the sensitivity of its receptors to that level.

An interesting point about serotonin, norepinephrine, acetylcholine, and to some degree dopamine, is that they tend to be "sprayed out" in a very general manner throughout the brain, by their presynaptic neurons. These transmitters, to some degree, are not very precisely released in terms of their location and timing. This stands in contrast to glutamate and GABA, which tend to be released in a more specific, point-for-point manner, in both space and time, within brain circuits. Thus, the modulatory transmitters may have effects that encompass a wide range of brain circuits and functions. Taking serotonin as an example, there is no *a priori* reason for thinking that it should only be involved in regulating depression (although we don't know exactly where the mood circuits are in the brain), since it is dispersed throughout the brain. Consistent with this notion, serotonin affects a broad range of brain functions and behavioral characteristics, such as mood, anxiety, impulsivity, short-term memory, cognitive flexibility, and self-esteem. So we shouldn't pigeonhole serotonin as being exclusively a mood or depression-related transmitter.

Another interesting point about serotonin is that brain imaging data suggest men generate about 50% higher brain levels of it than women do. Perhaps this finding is related to the well-established phenomenon that women have higher rates of major depression than men. To my knowledge, there are no brain imaging data on gender differences for norepinephrine (because the technology for measuring this may not yet exist), although in my previous book I put forth the theory that women tend to have higher brain levels of norepinephrine than men. Perhaps serotonin and norepinephrine play general roles in masculinity and femininity, possibly by affecting lateralized functions of the brain, with men being more "right brained" and women more "left brained".

The neurotransmitter acetylcholine has probably received a lot less attention than serotonin and norepinephrine, both among scientists and the general public, with regard to mental health. It may be an historical accident that acetylcholine is not thought of as being a lot like serotonin, including in regard to treating major depression with pharmaceutical drugs. If cholinesterase inhibitor drugs had come into prominence before Prozac and other SSRIs were invented, we may think of the neurochemistry of depression in particular and mental illness in general very differently. As I mentioned above, acetylcholine and serotonin may both be essentially inhibitory transmitters, and they have a similar widespread dispersal in the brain. Acetylcholine has been associated more so with cognition (that is, thinking and reasoning), whereas serotonin is more closely linked with mood, but they may each affect both properties and many more, and existing drugs that boost either transmitter may have similar neural and behavioral effects. This is an area of neuroscience and pharmacology that would greatly benefit from further investigation by scientists.

CHAPTER 4

Neurotransmitter imbalance theories and beyond

How does basic knowledge of neurotransmitter systems and their corresponding molecular pathways inside of cells, outlined in the previous chapter, translate into effects on mental health? This chapter will address this question, while also outlining evidence that certain aspects of mental illness may have nothing at all to do with transmitter systems. Let's begin with some older theories about what causes mood disorders, including major depression and bipolar disorder.

The 1950s and 1960s were groundbreaking decades for pharmaceutical treatment of mental illness, since many new psychiatric drugs with unprecedented mechanisms of action were being invented by scientists. Many of these drugs are still in widespread use today, including the tricyclic antidepressants (named for their three-ringed molecular structure), which are now largely thought to boost serotonin and/or norepinephrine, depending on the particular drug, by blocking reuptake of these transmitters from the synapse. A less widely used category of antidepressants, the monoamine oxidase inhibitors (MAO inhibitors, for short), was also invented in this time period, and these drugs are now thought to interfere with the breakdown of serotonin, norepinephrine, and dopamine, thereby enhancing their synaptic levels.

While these new drugs were being created, scientists around the world were intensively trying to figure out how they worked, as this was a mystery at the time (and to some degree it still is) Around this time, future Nobel Prize laureate Julius Axelrod at the National Institutes of Health in the United States, found that some tricyclic antidepressants interfere with norepinephrine reuptake, thereby increasing the synaptic level of this transmitter. As it became clearer that antidepressants may achieve their therapeutic effects by boosting the biogenic amines—serotonin, norepinephrine, and dopamine—Joseph Schildkraut at Harvard put forth in 1965 the so-called catecholamine hypothesis of mood disorders, where this fancy term refers to norepinephrine and dopamine. Schildkraut thought that these two transmitters may form, at least in part, a basis for depression and mania, where mania refers to the "high" state that persons with bipolar disorder may experience periodically. Schildkraut suggested that low levels of catecholamines may produce depression, and high levels mania. In 1967, Alec Coppen in the United Kingdom suggested similar ideas about serotonin, with emphasis on depression, where this became known as the indoleamine hypothesis of mood disorders (since serotonin is technically known as an indoleamine). In 1972, David Janowsky and colleagues in the United States expanded on these ideas in a lesser known hypothesis, suggesting that the balance of acetylcholine and norepinephrine in the brain governs mood disorders, with a high ratio of acetylcholine to norepinephrine producing depression, and a low ratio producing mania. I added my two cents to these ideas in a 2013 paper in which I suggested that *high* levels of serotonin, norepinephrine, and dopamine may produce depression, in addition to helping produce mania or mixtures of depression and mania. In summary, a number of so-called chemical imbalance theories have been put forth to explain the origins of depression and mania.

Elaborating upon these chemical imbalance ideas, I suggested in my previous book, *Adjust Your Brain*, that imbalance of serotonin and norepinephrine in particular forms the principal neurochemical basis of most mental illnesses, where differences in the brain circuitry with which these transmitters interact yields differences in the type of mental illness produced by the same underlying imbalance. One possibility is that most people are low in serotonin and/or high in norepinephrine signaling, where this imbalance may characterize all of Peter Kramer's case studies described earlier, and is a recurring theme within this book. Other researchers and doctors, such as Michael Norden, have suggested that many people may be low in serotonin. I'm suggesting not only that but also many people tend to be high in norepinephrine. If so, boosting serotonin and/or reducing norepinephrine with two separate drugs might improve the mental health of the vast majority of persons with mental illness, while also improving mental health for people who border on being mentally ill. I also stated in my previous book that far fewer people are pathologically high in serotonin and/or low in norepinephrine, and that a minority of people already have optimal mental health. Published data from studies on the genetics of the serotonin reuptake "pump" may indeed suggest that few people are high in serotonin, although this is an area of active research. I now think that dopamine and acetylcholine, in addition to serotonin and norepinephrine, play a prominent role in mental illness, and these ideas will be discussed further in the coming chapters.

The theories of Schildkraut, Coppen, and other scientists—collectively known as biogenic amine or monoamine theories of mood disorders—are widely known but have been highly criticized as being an oversimplification that is either incomplete or simply incorrect. One criticism involves explaining why monoaminergic antidepressants such as Prozac boost synaptic levels of monoamines within *minutes to hours* after taking them, yet these antidepressants typically require about two weeks to begin having therapeutic effects on depression. Perhaps these drugs, by boosting neurotransmitters, affect "downstream" molecular pathways including cAMP or induce neurogenesis (that is, birth of new neurons), which requires several weeks to take effect. Pharmaceutical companies, such as those that manufacture and market the SSRIs, have been attacked for advertising the "myth" that a chemical imbalance of these transmitters underlies depression, bipolar disorder, and other mental illnesses. While these criticisms of the biogenic amine hypothesis have merit and should be carefully considered, it is interesting to note that there actually are a number of studies that have measured the biogenic amines—in brain fluid, blood plasma, or urine—in persons with mood disorders and found that they often do appear to be altered in depression or mania. Eminent psychiatric researchers Frederick Goodwin and Kay Jamison, in their textbook on bipolar disorder, summarize these data, showing that mental illness may indeed involve a "chemical imbalance", at least in some persons. Renowned Yale psychiatric researcher, Amy Arnsten, has also suggested that optimal levels of monoamines, such as norepinephrine and dopamine, in prefrontal cortex may be necessary for optimal mental health, including our ability to store short-term memories and pay attention to things that are of interest.

Much like serotonin and norepinephrine have been strongly implicated in imbalance theories of depression, dopamine has been labeled a causative factor in schizophrenia in popular theories. These ideas can be traced to the same productive period for psychopharmacology in the 1950s and 1960s, when the first drugs with antipsychotic efficacy, such as Haldol and Thorazine, were being created. In the years that followed, when scientists determined that the ability of these and related drugs to block the dopamine D_2 receptor correlated with their ability to reduce or terminate psychosis (that is, hallucinations, delusions, and thought disorder) in persons with schizophrenia, the "dopamine hypothesis of schizophrenia" was born. As in the biogenic amine theories of mood disorders, the dopamine hypothesis of schizophrenia has strengths and weaknesses, and may complement other theories that I will describe below. Biogenic amine theories of practically every other mental illness, such as serotonin being implicated in autism or personality disorders, have also been put forth.

*   *   *

An exciting development in psychiatric drug treatment that has occurred in the last decade or so is the discovery that the "dissociative" (that is, reality distorting) anesthetic and drug of abuse, ketamine, has quickly-acting antidepressant properties in depressed persons. This finding is of high interest to psychiatry because the field has been searching for more rapidly-acting antidepressants, since monoaminergic drugs such as Prozac typically require several weeks to begin having a therapeutic effect. Ketamine, which blocks the NMDA receptor for the neurotransmitter glutamate (mentioned in the last chapter), appears to produce antidepressant effects within *hours* of intravenous administration. This finding not only may implicate glutamate signaling in depression, but also is highly surprising given the strangeness of the drug ketamine, which can be used to essentially mimic the symptoms of schizophrenia. Ketamine is closely related to another drug of abuse, PCP, which is also known as "angel dust". Pharmaceutical companies are very interested in these developments and some glutamate-related drugs are in development for potential use in humans. Since ketamine blocks the NMDA receptor and can produce symptoms that resemble schizophrenia, scientists have theorized that hypofunction (that is, reduced activity) of the brain's glutamate-related NMDA receptors plays a causative role schizophrenia.

Other non-biogenic amine drugs have been considered as alternative antidepressants or investigated for use in other clinical applications. This includes drugs that interact with peptide transmitter receptors, such as neuropeptide y. One intriguing drug, which ties in with our earlier discussion of the signaling molecule cAMP, is called rolipram. This drug does not regulate the *production* of cAMP, but rather interferes with its breakdown, thereby potentially boosting the level of cAMP inside the cell. Rolipram may have effects on various psychiatric disorders, including major depression, and this is an area of active research.

*   *   *

While theories that relate directly with neurotransmitter signaling pathways are critical to understanding psychiatric disorders as well as the drugs that modulate these disorders, these pathways are clearly not the whole story in mental illness. Several other brain mechanisms or therapeutic approaches, examples of which will be described below, may play an important role in mental health, including: hippocampal neurogenesis, the default mode network, stress-related effects on the structure of neurons, and deep brain stimulation of particular brain regions.

Until the 1990s, it was widely believed that adult humans are not able to generate new neurons. Through the efforts of eminent neuroscientist Fred Gage at the Salk Institute in California and other scientists, this idea has since been shown incorrect. Not only are adult humans, and various adult animals such as rodents and monkeys, capable of growing new neurons, this phenomenon may actually have effects on our mood. The hippocampus, a c-shaped structure that is present on both sides of the brain and that is strongly implicated in the formation and storage of memories through interaction with other parts of the brain, is now thought to also regulate whether we are depressed or not. Pioneering neuroscientist Rene Hen at Columbia University in New York, as well as other scientists, have shown that antidepressant drugs may boost mood in part by stimulating growth of new neurons in the hippocampus.

Another aspect of brain function that has garnered increasing interest in recent years is the so-called default mode network. This term refers to a group of functionally intertwined brain regions that tend to be most active when we are daydreaming or "spacing out". Marcus Raichle and co-workers from Washington University at Saint Louis identified this network of brain areas through functional brain imaging techniques, and have shown that it comes online when the brain is essentially idling. For our purposes, the default mode network is of high interest because scientific data suggest that it becomes more active in mental illnesses such as major depression. While the prevailing view of this network may be that greater activation of it is pathological, another possibility is that it can stimulate rumination and otherwise thinking about things that may serve various purposes. Another important point about the default mode network is that measuring it with functional brain imaging techniques may provide an objective "readout" of how depressed or otherwise mentally ill a given person is, while perhaps also indicating whether the person naturally shows a tendency toward rumination.

Exposure to significant psychological stress, such as being a victim of physical abuse, has long been thought to be a causative factor in mental illnesses such as major depression. While this idea has been linked with dysregulation of brain monoamine signaling, a more recent finding in the scientific literature, particularly in rodent studies, is that psychological stress can alter the very structure of neurons. Neuroscientists such as Andrew Holmes at the National Institutes of Health in the United States have shown that exposing animals even to a brief stressor can alter the anatomical structures of neurons in the prefrontal cortex and elsewhere in the brain. These structural changes can affect the dendritic branches of neurons, which are tree-like structures that receive synaptic input from other neurons. Determining the relative importance of anatomical changes in the brain that may result in depression in humans is an area of active research, and a topic discussed in Peter Kramer's book, *Against Depression*. Remodeling of neurons after exposure to stress may also relate to the phenomenon of hippocampal neurogenesis described above, in part because stress may affect neurons in the hippocampus.

Another pioneer in the field of neuroscience is Helen Mayberg of Emory University in Atlanta. She has been at the forefront of using a technique called deep brain stimulation to treat persons with intractable cases of major depression. Deep brain stimulation involves surgically implanting an electrode in a known brain target, through which electrical stimulation can be transmitted to neurons or neuronal fibers in the targeted region. More is probably known about using this technique to stimulate brain regions in Parkinson's disease to facilitate movement in persons who are having trouble getting around or controlling their movements. Mayberg has been among the first to use the technique in depressed persons, where the people in her studies typically failed to respond to a number of conventional treatments, including a variety of antidepressant drugs. In her hands and those of her co-workers, deep brain stimulation has often helped these persons, while also providing clues as to the brain circuits involved in regulation of mood. One brain region that has been targeted in deep brain stimulation of depression is called area 25, located toward the front of the brain. There are of course drawbacks in treating depression with surgical implantation of an electrode in the brain, including the potential long-term consequences of this invasive procedure, but it remains a fascinating and potentially critically important approach toward relieving depression in difficult to treat cases.

CHAPTER 5

Better than well in action

Now that we've discussed neurotransmitter systems and a number of related theories of mental illness, how does all of this relate to the central question of this book: how do we render someone better than well? The theories we've considered typically relate more to making someone who is mentally ill simply "well", rather than better than well, where the latter hasn't been frequently considered by most scientists or doctors. It's not so much that these theories would deny that better than well exists, but rather that these theorists never considered that it does. In subsequent chapters I will consider how to produce better than well in particular mental illnesses, as well as in persons who border on being mentally ill.

If better than well does indeed exist, and we want to implement it anytime soon, we need to work with the techniques we already have: pharmaceutical drugs, talk therapy, deep brain stimulation, electroconvulsive therapy (that is, shock therapy), transcranial magnetic stimulation, and vagal nerve stimulation, among others. The focus in this book is on pharmaceutical drugs, where I use the term "pharmaceutical" to signify those man-made drugs that are typically not abused by persons. In spite of the wide range of theories on mental illness that I've presented thus far, it may still be most effective to use variants of the chemical imbalance theories in deciding how to render people better than well by balancing these systems with existing drugs. This approach may be effective partly because the biogenic amine transmitters appear to play such a prominent, widespread role in brain function.

Implementing better than well outcomes using talk therapy could be the subject of a library full of books. I would simply like to state here that as with using drugs to treat mental illness, psychotherapy is still an area of active research and optimal use of its potentially very helpful treatments probably remains to be discovered, although in its current forms it can already be very helpful. Another point on psychotherapy, which may be related to Peter Kramer's ideas on psychopharmacology, is that perhaps it can be "cosmetic", by reshaping to the outward demeanor of the person and affecting his social interactions. If so, one question is whether psychotherapy also fundamentally alters the inner experience of the individual.

As mentioned earlier, we can draw an analogy between monoaminergic drugs correcting the brain equivalent of blurry vision in mental illness, and in doing so these drugs may act like "eyeglasses" or "contact lenses". To extend the analogy, might some future treatment of mental illness act like a "lasik procedure", in that we could correct the brain abnormality permanently, without need for ongoing treatment with drugs? For example, there is a drug called DSP-4 that can destroy a portion of norepinephrine neurons when given to animals. As I've suggested above, if many people have too much norepinephrine, might this drug or a similar one, or some more advanced technology, eventually be used to render people better than well on a permanent basis?

One issue about implementing better than well in a given person is simply verifying that it has indeed been produced. Observable behavior, or a person's outward appearance, which psychiatrists use to monitor how a person is reacting to a drug treatment, is often not a reliable indicator of his or her internal state, including mood. Having an objective marker, also known as an endophenotype or biomarker in scientific jargon, for better than well, such as through brain imaging, may help to implement it. Recall that we discussed previously that measuring activity in the default mode network, through such technologies as functional

MRI, may provide an objective marker of the intensity of depression or other mental illness. Likewise, measuring activation in and around area 25, where Helen Mayberg and colleagues have been providing deep brain stimulation, may also provide an objective marker of depression and possibly better than well effects.

*   *   *

A central point in this book is that better than well may become larger in magnitude and easier to produce in a given person if we can make more effective use of existing pharmaceutical drugs. This issue is especially important considering that in the last few years, Big Pharma companies have dramatically reduced their efforts to produce new psychiatric drugs. This flameout in interest was preceded by a number of high profile candidate drugs failing during late clinical trial testing. Even with the help of Big Pharma, preclinical research, which includes largely rodent-based research for psychiatric disorders, isn't always very efficient at translating basic findings into real world treatments for people. Hence the National Institutes of Health in the United States recently created a translational institute, aimed at making this process more efficient and more generally effective.

Existing drugs such as Prozac might be used more effectively by not only using the correct dose for a given person, but also by waiting longer for these drugs to reach maximum effect. The conventional wisdom is that monoaminergic drugs require several months to reach maximum therapeutic effect, but I believe they may actually take a number of years to do so. Another potentially critically important strategy in making better use of existing drugs is by more frequently using drugs that diminish norepinephrine signaling, since many people may have elevated signaling in this transmitter system. Very few studies, in humans or in animals, have examined the effect of increasing serotonin signaling with one drug and simultaneously lowering norepinephrine signaling with another. On a more general note, there are already drugs that raise or lower the levels of the serotonin, norepinephrine, and dopamine. Or that raise the level of acetylcholine or block its receptors. There is also a wide array of receptor subtype specific drugs that act on these four transmitters.

As we touched upon earlier, there is serendipity and randomness in the sequence in which different psychiatric drugs were created and came into prominent use. The field of medicine then became entrenched in using certain drugs, or classes of drugs, for particular disorders. Outside of the box thinking is typically not something that doctors put into practice when prescribing drugs for patients, partly due to the potential legal ramifications for them if something goes wrong. So the field of psychiatry (and neurology) may need to re-evaluate the manner in which it uses its various drugs, if better treatment for patients is to follow.

If we want people to use psychiatric drugs at all when there is a good reason to do so, one challenge we may face as a society is decreasing the stigma associated with their use. Many of us may be inherently skeptical or even afraid of using pharmaceutical drugs that affect the brain, and we may think that using them is therefore wrong. Another factor that may contribute to stigma is that, as described earlier, Big Pharma companies which produce many of these drugs have been vilified in recent years. To paraphrase a famous playwright: drugs are neither good nor bad, but thinking (or marketing) makes them so. In other words, through their association with Big Pharma, drugs are generally thought of in a negative fashion by much of the public, at least in the United States.

Marcia Angell, author of *The Truth About the Drug Companies: How They Deceive Us and What to Do About It*, has jumped on the bandwagon of attacking these companies. One point she makes is that these companies generally just crank out so-called me-too drugs, which are minor variations on existing drugs at the molecular level, that she thinks serve no or very little purpose for the public. She is incorrect in this argument; me-too drugs do serve at least one important medical purpose. Taking the SSRIs as an example of me-too drugs that were created after Prozac came out, these various other drugs—including Zoloft, Paxil, Celexa, Lexapro, and Luvox—are each effective for some persons where other drugs in the class are not effective for the given individual. In other words, a Prozac non-responder person with depression may instead respond to Zoloft, probably because at the molecular level, the key fits the lock for the serotonin reuptake transporter for the Zoloft molecule in this individual.

As we discuss particular mental illnesses in the following chapters, one age-old question in psychiatry is explaining the observation that the various mental illnesses often co-occur in the same person, frequently enough that this cannot be explained by chance. Various psychiatric disorders may also share genetic underpinnings. Moreover, psychiatric disorders often co-occur with neurological disorders such as Alzheimer's disease or epilepsy, as well as with non-psychiatric disorders such as diabetes or heart disease. One explanation for this may be that the same underlying factor or factors are causing multiple disorders. The monoamines may be good candidates for playing this role, especially considering the broad effectiveness of drugs such as Prozac that act on the biogenic amines, and that they are distributed throughout the brain and could thereby affect a number of psychiatric disorders. Norepinephrine and acetylcholine in particular are essentially dispersed throughout the body, and could thereby affect a number of diseases outside the brain as well.

* * *

Irving Kirsch of Harvard University, author of *The Emperor's New Drugs: Exploding the Antidepressant Myth*, is a prominent skeptic in the field of psychopharmacology today. Kirsch not only thinks that antidepressant drugs such as Prozac do not render people better than well, but also that these drugs will not even make them well, having barely any effect that is distinguishable from a placebo (that is, a pill with no drug). Kirsch has reached this conclusion by analyzing large numbers of so-called placebo-controlled studies, where the persons do not know if they are receiving a pill which contains drug, or instead a pill without drug. It is well known that placebos can have large psychological effects on a person, since the individual thinks he may actually be receiving an active drug that may be already known to produce psychiatric effects. Through his analysis of the data, Kirsch thinks that drugs such as Prozac either produce no therapeutic effect at all beyond that of a placebo, or only a very weak effect.

In support of Kirsch's ideas, it is actually difficult to completely rule out the possibility psychiatric drugs only produce placebo effects, even though there is a mountain of evidence they do more than this. Part of the problem is even though countless placebo-controlled studies support the idea antidepressants, and psychiatric drugs in general, have tangible effects in mentally ill persons, this could be related to persons in many of these studies knowing they are on drug rather than placebo due to various side effects such as nausea only a drug would probably produce. "Active" placebos, which contain substances that mimic the side effects of the drug, help to reduce this problem, but studies that use them are, to my knowledge, rarely carried out.

In support of psychiatric drugs having non-placebo-related, tangible effects on mental health, we may cite a number of lines of evidence: 1) animal studies of depression and anxiety-like behavior carried out in a "placebo" controlled manner, where animals either receive a drug injection or an inactive injection, 2) antidepressants produce transient perceptual changes in humans that would not easily be equated with a placebo effect, 3) drugs of abuse act on many of the same neurotransmitter systems as pharmaceutical psychiatric drugs, and few would argue drugs of abuse have no psychological effects, 4) human studies have shown measurable effects on behavior in "active" placebo controlled studies, 5) well-documented induction of mania in persons with bipolar disorder by antidepressant drugs, 6) even Peter Kramer's case studies may provide some evidence here: what kind of placebo effect would make a person less interested in viewing pornography? In other words, we may attribute increased happiness or giddiness as being a placebo effect produced when someone knows he's taking an antidepressant, but why would a person on such a drug exhibit non-mood-related changes in behavior as a placebo effect, such as increased assertiveness as described earlier?

CHAPTER 6

Depression and bipolar disorder

How might we render someone with unipolar depression or bipolar disorder better than well? (Note: "unipolar" refers to depression that is not accompanied by the "highs" that occur in bipolar disorder, which are called hypomania or mania. Hypomania is a milder form of full-blown mania.) As in the chapters that follow on various mental illnesses, the intention here is to present cutting edge information that would not only make persons with depression or bipolar disorder well, but hopefully better than well.

An issue we must face for these two disorders, as well as for other mental illnesses, is whether persons who develop mental illness at some point in life were once "normal"? Is there such a thing as "normal", or does everyone simply reside somewhere in a range between very healthy and very sick? I would suggest the range theory is correct, and there are data that support this view. For example, attention deficit hyperactivity disorder (ADHD) appears to exist as a range in the population of children, based on direct measures of hyperactivity. If mental illness exists as a range, perhaps a person who becomes severely ill may still retain some aspects of the illness, possibly in a changed form, after being rendered better than well. For example, perhaps someone who was highly paranoid while very ill may simply be very cautious about her safety after being rendered well or better than well.

In addition to describing conventional drug treatment strategies for unipolar depression and bipolar disorder, I have three major points to make in this chapter that describe largely novel, theoretical pharmaceutical approaches to treating these disorders: 1) reduce norepinephrine transmission, 2) enhance acetylcholine transmission as an alternative to using SSRIs or in addition to using them, 3) wait much longer than a few months to let monoaminergic drugs reach maximum effect. Since these are not widely known or highly studied treatment methods, they can be thought of as alternative approaches to treating these disorders, to be considered when conventional pharmaceutical approaches have failed or are inadequate. For now, more research and testing will need to be conducted to determine if these approaches are safe and effective. Let me begin by describing some more conventional pharmaceutical treatment strategies for rendering persons well or better than well.

Most of the commonly used antidepressants are thought to boost serotonin, norepinephrine, or both transmitters. While this does not necessarily indicate that reduced levels of these transmitters *causes* depression, it is consistent with this view. Since exposure to significant psychological stress is associated with producing depression, and animal studies show that serotonin and norepinephrine are released in large quantities as a result of stress, perhaps their levels are depleted thereafter, resulting in depression. There are three categories of widely used antidepressants: SSRIs such as Prozac; serotonin-norepinephrine reuptake inhibitors (SNRIs) such as Effexor and Cymbalta, which are thought to boost both serotonin and norepinephrine; and tricyclic antidepressants, some of which boost norepinephrine, others serotonin, and some boost both. Monoamine oxidase inhibitor drugs also boost monoamines, and are used to treat depression, but they are not as commonly prescribed because some of them can produce serious side effects. Remeron and Wellbutrin are two other commonly used antidepressants that may also act on monoamine signaling.

Since many antidepressants affect serotonin, norepinephrine, or both transmitters, a critical issue still facing psychiatry is whether it is a better strategy to boost only one or the other in a given depressed person, or instead to boost both. The conventional view in medicine these days may be that it is better to boost both, using an SNRI such as Effexor or Cymbalta, or by using two drugs at once. I would suggest here that a better strategy, which relates to our earlier discussion on serotonin and norepinephrine possibly counteracting one another in some ways in the brain, would be to boost only one of these transmitter systems with a single drug. SSRIs in general (where Lexapro is the most selective of these) specifically boost serotonin. Certain tricyclic antidepressants (desipramine, nortriptyline) and two other antidepressants (reboxetine, atomoxetine) selectively boost norepinephrine.

If it really is better to boost just one of these two transmitters in treating depression, an additional question is of course which one to boost in a given person? As I've suggested earlier, serotonin deficiency may be more common than norepinephrine deficiency, so one strategy could be to try boosting serotonin first in a given person, and if that is ineffective then try boosting norepinephrine. In spite of the possibility that serotonin and norepinephrine offset one another in some ways, SNRIs can nonetheless be very effective in treating depression, possibly because they only boost one of these transmitters in a given person, or because they boost both, where serotonin and norepinephrine act cooperatively in some ways.

A related point, described in *Listening to Prozac*, is that tricyclic antidepressants or norepinephrine boosting drugs in general may be more effective than SSRIs for treating severe depression, also known as melancholic depression. This remains an open and understudied question, and in my opinion some cases of severe depression may respond better to SSRIs than to norepinephrine boosting drugs. As also pointed out by Peter Kramer, the monoamine oxidase inhibitor drugs may boost serotonin more so than norepinephrine, or at least resemble SSRIs more than they do tricyclic antidepressants in their behavioral effects.

Another issue we face in treating depression is whether different strategies should be used for the various putative subtypes of the disorder, including atypical depression. This subtype of depression is characterized by oversleeping and overeating, the opposite of the more widely known symptoms of the disease where persons have insomnia and lack much of an appetite. In a theoretical scientific paper published in 2013, I suggested that atypical depression is caused, at least in part, by elevated norepinephrine signaling. There are a few reasons for thinking so. One is that there is evidence elevated norepinephrine signaling may increase appetite and lead to overeating, whether a person is depressed or not. Another reason elevated norepinephrine may help cause atypical depression is that a person's sleep characteristics may be an indicator of the status of his monoamines. There is evidence that the synaptic levels of serotonin and norepinephrine build as the day wears on, and are removed from the synapse during sleep. I think that sleep regulates the levels of the monoamines: if serotonin or norepinephrine is too low, we sleep less, so as to not further reduce the levels; if these monoamines are too high, we sleep more, to reduce their high levels. So depressions characterized by premature awakening or insomnia in general may be caused in part by too low a level of serotonin or norepinephrine. Depressions characterized by oversleeping, as in atypical depression, may be partially caused by too high a level of serotonin or norepinephrine, where I think atypical depression involves elevated norepinephrine. Consistent with this theory, a fairly recent study of atypical depression found that this disorder responds better to a serotonin boosting antidepressant than it does to a norepinephrine boosting one.

The idea that our sleep patterns regulate levels of the monoamines in the brain may be related to another aspect of depressive disorders, including but not limited to atypical depression: so-called diurnal (that is, within a day) patterns in depression. It is well known that for some persons with depression, they feel worse in the morning and better as the day wears on; others with depression feel better in the morning and worse as the day wears on. As mentioned above, if serotonin and norepinephrine tend to build as the day wears on, then perhaps depressions that get better as evening approaches are characterized by too low a level of serotonin or norepinephrine, whereas depressions that are worse by evening may involve too high a level of serotonin or norepinephrine. Another factor in these diurnal patterns is the stress hormone cortisol, which may be functionally related to norepinephrine, and whose regulation is known to be disrupted in depression.

As stated earlier, I think most people with depression or bipolar disorder, and even most people with no overt mental illness, have low serotonin and/or high norepinephrine signaling (that is, they either have both of these abnormalities, or only one of them), mainly through genetics but also as a result of life experiences, including exposure to psychological stress. A minority of persons with depression or bipolar disorder may instead have elevated serotonin and/or lowered norepinephrine. One reason for thinking so involves a gene that regulates the expression of the serotonin reuptake transporter in the brain. The variants of this gene in the human population suggest that more people have high expression of the transporter, which would probably produce low levels of synaptic serotonin. People who have low expression of the transporter and therefore may have elevated serotonin transmission should not, in my opinion, be given SSRIs to treat depression or other mental illness, although this is a controversial issue among psychiatric researchers.

One of the mysteries involving monoaminergic antidepressants is why they seem to require several weeks to begin working in most people with depression who take them, even though these drugs boost serotonin and/or norepinephrine essentially immediately. Catherine Harmer, Philip Cowen, and colleagues at Oxford University in England have performed a series of pioneering studies using antidepressants and related drugs that act on serotonin or norepinephrine, which indicate that these drugs bias emotional processing in humans so as to produce, in some ways at least, a more favorable or positive outlook. Surprisingly, this "rose colored glasses" effect occurs within minutes or hours of taking these drugs, even though a person's mood is not altered this quickly. Harmer and Cowen think that antidepressants subtly yet quickly begin to shift a depressed person's negative outlook to a more positive one, and within a week or two this revised outlook begins to result in a lifting of the depressed mood.

An important issue in treating depression and bipolar disorder with existing drugs is that people often appear to respond to certain drugs and not to others. For example, within the class of SSRIs, it is well known that some persons may not show any therapeutic response to one drug, while showing a robust response to another. So just because the first several drugs do not work well for a given person, this does not mean that subsequent ones also will not. A few years ago, a large study called Sequenced Treatment Alternatives to Relieve Depression (STAR*D, for short) was carried out to assess the value of switching drugs when the first one does not work or only produces a weak response. This study concluded that there indeed can be a benefit in switching drugs, even several times, in such cases.

*　　*　　*

I have included both unipolar depression and bipolar disorder in the same chapter not only because both disorders can involve depression, but also because they may share similar underlying monoamine chemistry. A recurring theme in this book, as well as in my previous one, is that most mental illnesses, including unipolar depression and bipolar disorder, are usually characterized by weak serotonin and/or strong norepinephrine signaling. The reason various mental illnesses can share similar underlying neurochemistry yet nonetheless appear to be different disorders may be because the brain circuitry with which the monoamines interact varies in different individuals, partly due to genetics. Another factor that may distinguish unipolar depression from bipolar disorder is the neurotransmitter dopamine, which may tend to be more elevated in the latter disorder.

In treating the depressive phase of bipolar disorder, it is considered controversial to add antidepressant drugs to the standard mood stabilizing drugs that are used to treat the disorder. Antidepressants can induce hypomania or mania in persons with bipolar disorder, as well as rapid cycling of mood, whether the person suffers from bipolar II disorder or bipolar I, where the latter is considered the more severe subtype. My opinion on this topic is that generally antidepressants should be avoided in bipolar disorder, especially if the person is already cycling up and down without them. However, if a particular case is characterized by significant depression that does not appear to be remitting spontaneously after extended periods of time (such as a number of months), an antidepressant should be considered, but only in conjunction with a mood stabilizer. In this scenario, it can be tricky to find the correct doses of both the antidepressant and mood stabilizer; one strategy is to minimize the dose of the antidepressant and maximize the dose of the mood stabilizer, to avoid marked cycling of mood.

Lithium was the first mood stabilizing drug to come into prominent use worldwide, where its calming effect on animals was discovered accidentally by an essentially unknown Australian psychiatrist named John Cade in 1949. It took decades before it became widely used, as the medical field was slow to adopt it. While lithium has saved and continues to save countless lives, it can also have nasty side effects, such as damaging the kidneys, and typically requires ongoing medical monitoring in its users. Other drugs with mood stabilizing properties, including anti-epilepsy drugs called anticonvulsants, which include carbamazepine and valproate among others, can also have significant side effects. The atypical antipsychotics, which block the serotonin 5-HT_{2A} and dopamine D_2 receptors, can also have significant side effects, including weight gain and induction of type 2 diabetes. One possibility is that lithium, the anticonvulsants, and even the atypical antipsychotics may all at least partially produce their therapeutic effects in bipolar disorder by reducing norepinephrine signaling or molecular pathways that are closely related to norepinephrine signaling.

Kay Jamison, the eminent writer and Johns Hopkins University psychiatric researcher who suffers from bipolar disorder herself, has gathered evidence that this disorder is more common in artists than in the general population, and I think this is correct. However, the more general hypothesis, as I argued in *Adjust Your Brain*, is that the prevalence of bipolar disorder in artists is a special case of a more general phenomenon in that nearly all artists have strong norepinephrine signaling. Such a neurotransmitter array may enhance sense of aesthetics. I also view bipolar disorder as being a largely genetic disease, which is characterized by elevated norepinephrine signaling in most persons who have it, and elevated serotonin signaling in a small proportion of persons.

Regarding implementing better than well treatment in persons with bipolar disorder, perhaps this would involve: 1) stopping their mood cycling altogether, 2) making their depressions less unpleasant and their hypomanias more pleasant. Producing point 1 may not be possible in most cases, especially in bipolar II disorder, so trying to implement point 2 may be the more feasible outcome.

*   *   *

Now that we've discussed some standard issues and approaches to treating unipolar depression and bipolar disorder, here are a few ideas for rendering people with these disorders better than well. This is not to suggest that standard treatments, such as using Prozac to treat depression, cannot already yield better than well results.

The ideas that follow are largely based in theory and require further scientific inquiry to be confirmed. One idea, which may be applicable to other mental illnesses as well, is that reducing norepinephrine signaling with existing pharmaceutical drugs may help treat many cases of unipolar depression, as well as bipolar disorder. While this is not a widely known treatment strategy for either disorder, there are a number of published scientific studies that support this approach. There are also plenty of drugs that either block norepinephrine receptors, including the beta receptor blocker propranolol and the alpha blocker prazosin, or that lower the level of synaptic norepinephrine (clonidine, guanfacine). Lowering norepinephrine signaling is not a widely used approach for treating depression or bipolar disorder, and implementing it could significantly improve mental health for a large number of persons. Also, if many people with these disorders have low serotonin signaling in addition to high norepinephrine signaling, using one drug (such as Prozac or Lexapro) to raise serotonin, while lowering norepinephrine signaling with a second drug, could synergistically improve treatment outcome.

An additional treatment approach that may help persons with unipolar depression or bipolar disorder is boosting the neurotransmitter acetylcholine with cholinesterase inhibitor drugs, such as galantamine and donepezil. This is not an established treatment method, but as I stated earlier there are theoretical reasons for thinking that boosting acetylcholine has a similar effect to boosting serotonin, and this may be an important alternative treatment when persons don't respond to SSRIs or have significant side effects when taking them. An additional question is whether cholinesterase inhibitors have synergistically beneficial effects when combined with SSRIs, and also whether the former drugs are especially beneficial when combined with norepinephrine reducing drugs.

One possibility regarding how SSRIs actually achieve their therapeutic effects on depression is that by boosting synaptic serotonin, they achieve a significant portion of their antidepressant effect by activating the 5-HT_{2C} receptor subtype. In my view, serotonin is a largely inhibitory neurotransmitter and the 5-HT_{2C} receptor is also largely inhibitory, whereas the 5-HT_{2A} subtype is largely excitatory. This line of reasoning may suggest that drugs which selectively activate the 5-HT_{2C} receptor would be effective antidepressants, and this is an area of active research, including by pharmaceutical companies.

A third experimental approach for maximizing the effects of existing pharmaceutical drugs when treating depression or bipolar disorder is simply to wait longer to let the drugs reach maximum therapeutic effect. There are theoretical and empirical reasons for believing that drugs which act on monoamines may take a number of *years* to reach maximum effect. Psychiatrists typically only wait a few months or less when deciding that these drugs, at a certain dose, have done all they can do to help a person, and then patient and doctor usually change things up. When a drug regimen appears to be having some benefit for a given person, a better strategy may be to wait longer and see if things improve further.

CHAPTER 7

Schizophrenia

Schizophrenia is one of the most devastating mental illnesses, both for those who suffer from it and for their family members. It is also the focus of intensive research, yet the conventional treatment methods which in part rely on psychiatric drugs often still leave the individual in a state in which he is not able to function normally. Revised treatment methods are sorely needed for this disease. Let me now briefly discuss some theories on the origins of schizophrenia, conventional pharmaceutical treatment strategies, and then some unconventional drug treatments that may help render people with this disorder better than well.

Probably the most widely known theory about what causes schizophrenia relates to abnormalities in signaling by the neurotransmitter, dopamine. This so-called "dopamine hypothesis of schizophrenia" was put forth no later than the 1970s, when it was discovered that antipsychotic drugs such as Haldol and Thorazine, which had first been generated by chemists in the 1950s, may achieve their therapeutic effects by blocking dopamine receptors in the brain. It was shown in the 1970s that effectiveness of these and related drugs at treating schizophrenia correlates directly with how well they block the D_2 dopamine receptor in particular, and hence the idea was born that schizophrenia is caused by elevated dopamine signaling through the D_2 receptor. Many variations of this "dopamine hypothesis" have been proposed since then, by such researchers as Solomon Snyder at Johns Hopkins University, Anthony Grace at the University of Pittsburgh, and Arvid Carlsson of the University of Gothenburg in Sweden, including that *reduced* dopamine signaling causes at least some cases or aspects of the disease.

Dopamine is not the only neurotransmitter that has been implicated in schizophrenia. The hallucinogenic street drug LSD has long been thought to model the symptoms of "madness" that occur in schizophrenia, although in some ways it may provide a poor model of the disorder. It is now widely believed that LSD and related hallucinogens achieve their psychedelic effects by activating the serotonin 5-HT_{2A} receptor (although they may also interact with 5-HT_{2C}), consistent with the 5-HT_{2A} receptor in particular and serotonin in general playing a role in schizophrenia. Adding further credibility to this line of reasoning, the antipsychotic drug clozapine is thought to mainly achieve its therapeutic effects by blocking the 5-HT_{2A} receptor rather than dopamine receptors.

A more recent theory about the cause of schizophrenia centers on the neurotransmitter, glutamate. Recall that this is the brain's most abundant excitatory transmitter, in that it tends to activate the electrical properties of neurons. One variant of glutamate theories of schizophrenia concerns the NMDA receptor, which is one of the prominent receptors for glutamate in the brain. The so-called "NMDA receptor hypofunction hypothesis of schizophrenia" suggests that underfunctioning of this important receptor subtype results in the disease. Consistent with this idea, the "dissociative" anesthetic drug ketamine, which is commonly abused by people, blocks the NMDA receptor and can mimic symptoms of schizophrenia.

A lesser known theory of schizophrenia suggests that elevated norepinephrine signaling is a cause of the disorder, particularly in the paranoid subtype of the illness. Part of the reason for thinking so is that some studies in humans have shown that norepinephrine transmission reducing drugs, such as the transmitter level lowering drug clonidine or the beta blocker propranolol, may help treat symptoms of the disease. An interesting fact about norepinephrine is that it is released in the brain and elsewhere in the body in response to stressful stimuli; it is known as a "stress hormone". Schizophrenia, along with just about every other mental illness, can be triggered or worsened, at least in part, by exposure to significant stressors. So it makes sense that norepinephrine may play a role in the disease. A less established idea is that *genetically* elevated norepinephrine signaling is a causative factor in schizophrenia. The idea that norepinephrine is a factor in schizophrenia may tie in with the observation that when pregnant mothers are exposed to significant stress, their children are more likely to develop the disease later in life.

The various theories of schizophrenia described above are not necessarily mutually exclusive, as each may apply in different individuals, or may combine in a given person. Regarding particular receptor subtypes and their effects on neural excitability, I think of the dopamine D_2 receptor (and dopamine itself) as inhibitory. And even though the overall effect of serotonin in the brain may be inhibitory, I think of the 5-HT_{2A} receptor as excitatory. On the other hand, the overall effect of glutamate in the brain is excitatory, although in a 2012 paper I suggested that the effect of the NMDA receptor is largely inhibitory. Norepinephrine, through its various postsynaptic receptors, may be primarily excitatory. In summary, two of these transmitters (but not necessarily all of their receptors) are excitatory and two inhibitory, suggesting that differences in brain circuits with which they interact may be the means through which they produce schizophrenia, rather than whether they (or their receptors) are in general excitatory or inhibitory.

* * *

Conventional treatments of schizophrenia rely heavily on use of so-called antipsychotic drugs, also known as neuroleptics. A more recently developed subset of these drugs is known as the atypical antipsychotics, including Zyprexa, Geodon, and several others, which have more selective effects on the dopaminergic system and tend to have fewer side effects. Use of older antipsychotic drugs, such as Haldol and Thorazine, is more likely to result in a potentially irreversible condition called tardive dyskinesia, which is characterized by various involuntary movements. Whereas the atypical antipsychotics are thought to largely produce their therapeutic effects by blocking both the D_2 and 5-HT_{2A} receptors, a lesser known finding with the older "typical" antipsychotics is that they not only block D_2 but also 5-HT_{2A} quite effectively. Persons with schizophrenia, in addition to experiencing so-called positive signs such as delusions, hallucinations, and disordered thinking and speech, may also experience so-called negative signs, including apathy and depression. The conventional wisdom is that the negative signs don't respond that well to antipsychotic drugs, so psychiatrists sometimes add antidepressant drugs to the treatment regimen. In summary, conventional treatments of schizophrenia rely heavily on antipsychotic drugs, especially the atypical antipsychotics these days, along with occasional add-on drugs such as antidepressants. Unfortunately, this treatment strategy is often not very effective, as many persons with schizophrenia remain incapacitated by the illness.

How might we go about rendering persons with schizophrenia better than well, or at least better than they usually become with conventional treatment methods? As stated earlier, I believe that most mental illnesses share similar neurotransmitter system abnormalities, which through interaction with brain circuitry that differs in various people results in presentation of different mental illnesses. I think most mental illnesses are characterized by weak serotonin signaling and/or strong norepinephrine transmission, and schizophrenia is no exception, although strong dopamine signaling may also play an important role in the illness.

So I'll now outline some largely theoretical principles for treating schizophrenia more effectively, which resemble the ideas presented for depression and bipolar disorder in the previous chapter: 1) reduce norepinephrine signaling, 2) raise serotonin or acetylcholine signaling, 3) wait longer for the psychiatric drugs to take full effect. These are not proven treatment methods, but there is evidence suggesting they may be valid, and they may complement standard antipsychotic drugs as add-on treatments.

Regarding reducing norepinephrine signaling, there are a number of drugs that either lower release of norepinephrine (clonidine, guanfacine, and others), or that block norepinephrine receptors (propranolol, prazosin, and others). There is evidence from human schizophrenia studies that at least some of these drugs have therapeutic efficacy in the disease (particularly in the paranoid subtype of the disorder), which may be comparable with standard antipsychotic drugs. There is also some evidence that antipsychotic drugs at least partially achieve their effects by lowering norepinephrine signaling.

As with raising serotonin or acetylcholine, the approach of lowering norepinephrine transmission could be achieved by adding such a drug to the standard antipsychotic drug regimen. In general, these theoretical suggestions listed here for instituting better than well treatment in schizophrenia may be best achieved by adding these treatments to more well established antipsychotic drug approaches, or as an alternative when the standard approaches have failed. A related point is that tricyclic antidepressants, many of which *boost* norepinephrine signaling, can increase suicidality in persons with schizophrenia, making it questionable as to whether tricyclics should ever be used in the disorder.

Another approach that may help institute better than well treatment in schizophrenia involves raising acetylcholine or serotonin signaling with existing drugs. A well known fact is that a very high fraction of persons with schizophrenia smoke cigarettes. Since nicotine in cigarettes activates nicotinic acetylcholine receptors, perhaps persons with the disorder are smoking to compensate for an acetylcholine deficiency (that is, self medicating), which may be treated in a more healthy and effective manner by taking a cholinesterase inhibitor drug. As stated earlier, acetylcholine may be very similar to serotonin in brain function, where both are essentially inhibitory neurotransmitters, so boosting serotonin with SSRI drugs may also be effective in schizophrenia. This latter point may seem to run contrary to the observation that *blocking* serotonin signaling at the excitatory 5-HT$_{2A}$ receptor helps treat the disorder, but here I am suggesting that an SSRI would activate signaling at a large range of other serotonin receptors which are mainly inhibitory. Combining the SSRI or cholinesterase inhibitor approach with additional drugs that lower norepinephrine signaling may have a synergistically beneficial effect in some cases of schizophrenia.

A third and final point on implementing better than well treatment in persons with schizophrenia involves waiting longer than several months to allow the various drug regimens to reach maximum therapeutic effect. As stated in the previous chapter, drugs that act on the modulatory neurotransmitters may take several years to reach maximum effect. This approach may apply both to the above better than well ideas for the disorder, as well as giving standard antipsychotic drug regimens longer to take full effect.

CHAPTER 8

Autism

Autism has been a popular topic in the news in recent years, with many parents fearing that their young children will receive this diagnosis. In its more severe forms, autism can be profoundly debilitating, intellectually and otherwise, although its milder forms such as Asperger syndrome may simply be normal variants of personality. Scientists and laypersons alike continue to identify candidate causes of autism, such as maternal exposure to toxic substances during pregnancy, or whether some type of virus causes the disorder. While I acknowledge that maternal exposure to psychological stress or perhaps various toxins during pregnancy may help eventually lead to the disorder in the child, here I suggest that the global brain signaling molecules that we've been discussing, including serotonin and norepinephrine, are the most likely candidates for causing autism.

One key question in treating autism with pharmaceutical drugs is whether it is principally a developmental disorder, wherein after the brain has developed to some degree in a child, the disorder can no longer be treated effectively with drugs. It may be that while intervening with treatments during pregnancy and in the first few years of life is important, a good deal can still be done about autism after it has developed, using various existing drugs. Perhaps the most well studied pharmaceutical treatment for autism, both in children and adults, is use of SSRIs, which may produce mild improvement in symptoms in the manner in which these drugs are typically used.

One debilitating aspect of autism is that persons who suffer from the disorder have trouble understanding the thoughts, emotions, and intentions of other people. This so-called Theory of Mind view of autism suggests that the disorder impairs the ability to "read minds", not in an astrological sense but in simply gauging what other people may be generally thinking about. The brain basis of this "mind blindness" phenomenon may be the result of deficits in prefrontal cortex functioning. This region of the brain plays a critical role in so-called executive functions, including our ability to interact socially with peers. A number of brain regions, many of which may interact with prefrontal cortex, are home to an intriguing set of cells called "mirror neurons", which may be present both in humans and in animals. These neurons become active both when an individual himself performs a particular action and when he sees someone else perform that action, and it is thought that these neural responses may be related to our sense of empathy.

An open area of inquiry in neuroscience research is whether neuromodulators such as serotonin and norepinephrine interact with the mirror neuron system. Trevor Robbins of the University of Cambridge and Amy Arnsten of Yale University, pioneering researchers in studies of prefrontal cortex, have shown that serotonin, norepinephrine, and related molecules—as well as drugs that act on these systems—can dramatically affect the functional properties of prefrontal cortex, as well as potentially altering its interaction with other brain regions. In 2011, I published a theoretical paper on this topic, suggesting that serotonin plays a general role in activating prefrontal cortex, whereas norepinephrine deactivates this brain region. A more refined theory may suggest that serotonin and norepinephrine have opposing effects on various subregions of prefrontal cortex, where some regions tend to be activated by serotonin and others by norepinephrine.

One poorly understood aspect of autism is that it can result in sensory abnormalities, including changes in hearing or touch, producing either heightened or deadened sensation. I suggested in my previous book that serotonin tends to deaden the five senses and norepinephrine tends to heighten them, so perhaps underlying brain abnormalities in these transmitter systems can produce sensory changes in autism. With norepinephrine being a putatively excitatory transmitter, and serotonin an inhibitory one, perhaps persons with autism who have enhanced musical abilities have more acute hearing as a result of elevated norepinephrine signaling, or a high ratio of norepinephrine to serotonin.

This last point may be related to the profound intellectual deficits and language delays that characterize some cases of autism: perhaps pathologically elevated neural excitability, resulting from a high ratio of norepinephrine to serotonin throughout the brain, impairs learning. This may partly be the case because the individual "cannot see the forest for the trees", for lack of filtering more important points from trivial details. On the other hand, sensitivity to detail and perhaps enhanced ability to remember things, may result in some of the savant-like, increased specific cognitive abilities in some persons with autism.

*   *   *

As stated above, probably the most well-established pharmaceutical treatment for autism is serotonin boosting with SSRIs, but these drugs appear to only have limited effects on the disorder. One possibility is that if these treatments were given to the mother during pregnancy or to the child very soon after birth, they may be more effective, but this may not be an entirely practical or safe approach to treating autism. So how might we render persons with this disorder better than well?

The ideas that follow are largely based in theory and require further scientific inquiry to be confirmed. I would suggest that autism is, in most cases at least, fundamentally a disorder of weak serotonin signaling and/or strong norepinephrine signaling, so similar principles may apply as were described above for depression, bipolar disorder, and schizophrenia: 1) lower norepinephrine transmission, 2) raise serotonin and/or acetylcholine signaling, 3) wait longer, possibly several years, for these drugs to take full effect. The first point can be accomplished through norepinephrine release lowering drugs such as clonidine and guanfacine, the beta blocker propranolol, or the alpha blocker prazosin. The second point relates to boosting serotonin with SSRIs and/or acetylcholine through cholinesterase inhibitors. Combining points one and two, for example by lowering norepinephrine transmission with clonidine, while raising serotonin with Prozac, may have a synergistically beneficial effect on autism. The third point suggests that conventional pharmaceutical approaches to treating autism with SSRIs or other drugs listed above typically only wait weeks to several months to allow these agents to reach maximum therapeutic effect, and this may not be nearly long enough. All three of these points, aside from use of SSRIs, represent unconventional approaches to treating autism that await further testing by future scientific studies.

CHAPTER 9

OCD

Obsessive-compulsive disorder, or OCD for short, is an anxiety disorder in which persons exhibit obsessive thinking patterns about particular topics, and then often feel compelled to engage in repetitive or ritualistic behaviors related to their obsessions. In a commonly used example of the illness, the individual fears contamination by germs to an exaggerated extent, and then engages in so much hand washing as to damage the skin on his hands. One topic that has been in the news in recent years is hoarding, where a person may fill her home from carpet to ceiling with unnecessary items, refusing to get rid of these things as they accumulate. Hoarding may be related to OCD, although some experts consider it a separate disorder.

As for autism, the most widely used pharmaceutical treatment for OCD is probably serotonin boosting, typically with SSRI drugs and often at high doses. SSRIs do have some degree of success in treating OCD, especially in particular cases. Recall that author Lauren Slater, who suffers from OCD, wrote in her wonderful book *Prozac Diary* that this drug is "Zen medicine". The brain basis of OCD, as for a number of other psychiatric disorders, may fundamentally relate to dysfunction in the prefrontal cortex, as well as in deeper brain structures called the basal ganglia (which are linked to habitual behavior and regulation of movement), or the functional balance between these large-scale regions of the brain.

This idea may tie in with a recurring theme in this book, and my previous one, that most people with mental illness have diminished serotonin signaling and/or enhanced norepinephrine transmission. In a theoretical paper that I published in 2011, I suggested that serotonin may play a general role in activating prefrontal cortex, whereas norepinephrine tends to deactivate this brain region. A related theory is that serotonin tends to *deactivate* the basal ganglia and norepinephrine *activates* this brain region. Hence these two transmitters may affect the balance between prefrontal cortex and the basal ganglia, with serotonin tending to shift the balance toward prefrontal cortex and norepinephrine shifting it away. A more refined view of the effects of these two transmitters is that whereas norepinephrine may deactivate much of prefrontal cortex, it may activate a particular subregion called orbitofrontal cortex that is linked with OCD.

How does all of this relate to OCD? The principal way is that, as mentioned earlier, the prefrontal cortex plays a key role in so-called executive functions, such as engaging in flexible, goal-directed behaviors. On the other hand, the basal ganglia may play a relatively greater role in promoting rigid, habitual behaviors, as opposed to goal-directed ones. OCD may principally result from overactive habitual circuitry in the brain, especially in terms of the basal ganglia, although an overactive orbitofrontal cortex may also play a role, according to brain imaging studies in humans. Overactive basal ganglia and orbitofrontal circuits may be the result of weakened serotonin signaling and/or heightened norepinephrine signaling, possibly due to genetics in the given person.

*   *   *

How might we go about rendering someone with OCD better than well with existing pharmaceutical drugs? The ideas presented on this topic in what follows are largely based in theory and require further scientific inquiry to be confirmed.

Conventional drug treatment for OCD tends to employ SSRIs such as Prozac (or the serotonin boosting drug, clomipramine), often given at high doses. How might we improve on this strategy? Not surprisingly, here I am suggesting that the same drug strategies put forth in the last several chapters may in theory improve effectiveness in OCD: 1) lower norepinephrine signaling, 2) raise serotonin and/or acetylcholine signaling, 3) wait longer than just a month or two to allow these drug regimens to reach maximum therapeutic effect. Following these three principles may produce a more healthy balance between activation of prefrontal cortex and the basal ganglia, and functional connectivity between these structures, thereby helping treat OCD more effectively.

To implement point 1 by lowering norepinephrine signaling, we could use drugs that either lower synaptic levels of norepinephrine (clonidine, guanfacine), block alpha receptors (prazosin), or block beta receptors (propranolol). All of these drugs penetrate the brain and have psychiatric effects, whereas many other norepinephrine based drugs, including a number of beta blockers, do not cross the blood-brain barrier to enter the brain. To implement point 2, we can raise serotonin signaling with SSRIs (Prozac, Zoloft, Paxil, Lexapro, Luvox) and/or raise acetylcholine with cholinesterase inhibitors (donepezil, galantamine, and others). Combining points one and two may suggest that lowering norepinephrine signaling with one drug, while raising serotonin/acetylcholine signaling with another may produce synergistically beneficial effects on OCD. Finally, point three above suggests that all of the drugs in this paragraph may actually take a very long time, such as several years, to reach full effect when give at a steady dose. Changing the dose more quickly than this, for a given drug, may not allow it to reach maximum effect.

CHAPTER 10

Drug and alcohol abuse

The conventional wisdom, outside of scientific circles, may be that anyone can succumb to drug or alcohol abuse, and that differences in life circumstances lead some people down this path. While it may be true that anyone can resort to substance abuse, scientific studies in animals and humans indicate that different individuals may be much more likely to do so than others, including through genetic variability among persons. Part of a genetic predisposition for substance abuse may be related to individual differences in the modulatory transmitter systems—serotonin, norepinephrine, dopamine, acetylcholine, and others.

Of the various neuromodulators that may affect substance abuse, dopamine has been most closely and extensively associated with brain "reward", which is a pleasurable response to various stimuli such as drugs. This is an idea that continues to be studied on a broad scale by researchers such as Nora Volkow at the National Institutes of Health in the United States. Norepinephrine may also play a prominent role in reward, including through activation of the orbitofrontal cortex, or a structure that is buried deeper in the brain, the nucleus accumbens. Dopamine and norepinephrine may interact in this role, including in prefrontal cortex and the nucleus accumbens. David Weinshenker and co-workers at Emory University have been carrying out pioneering work in norepinephrine for a number of years, including implicating this transmitter in reward.

Some of the effects of dopamine or norepinephrine on reward seeking in general, or substance abuse in particular, may be mediated by differences in human personality. A variety of personality types may be more predisposed to substance abuse than others: two examples are persons who are high in the stimulus or sensation seeking trait (that is, for example, thrill seeking types), or persons who are hypomanic (that is, who exhibit low level mania), where these personality traits may overlap in a given person. Stimulus seeking and hypomania may both be related to elevated levels of monoamines in the brain—serotonin, norepinephrine, and dopamine. The ideas of the eminent psychiatric researcher, C. Robert Cloninger, particularly implicate dopamine in stimulus or novelty seeking, and this transmitter is also strongly associated with hypomania. One possibility is that persons who experience hypomania, or bipolar disorder in general, attempt to regulate their moods through substance abuse: for example, trying to "take the edge off" a high by using a "downer" such as alcohol, or trying to feel better when depressed by taking an "upper" such as cocaine.

Mental illness in general, which is associated with high rates of substance abuse, may influence various factors that motivate a person to begin taking drugs and to keep taking them. One unifying factor by which the various mental illnesses may affect substance abuse is through "executive dysfunction" in prefrontal cortex, a topic we've discussed earlier. Since many psychiatric disorders are characterized by executive dysfunction, they may predispose a person to impulsive behavior, as well as producing a bias toward habitual actions such as drug abuse. Exposure to psychological stress, where stress is associated with increased release of norepinephrine in the brain and the rest of the body, is linked with substance abuse and also with executive dysfunction.

An idea that I have been developing in recent years is that elevated norepinephrine signaling—whether as a result of genetics, exposure to significant stress, or both—is a shared, major factor in a wide range of substance abuse disorders. The list of substances may include alcohol, marijuana, nicotine, heroin, synthetic opiates (such as Vicodin), cocaine, and even caffeine. One possibility is that these drugs tend to dampen elevated norepinephrine signaling, thereby producing a positive psychological effect in the user—that is, a "high". Moreover, this effect may be related to addiction, since when the user stops using these drugs, norepinephrine signaling overshoots and makes the person feel terrible and compelled to resume using the drug. A number of studies suggest, however, that these drugs may actually produce their "high" in part by *boosting* norepinephrine signaling, although they may be suppressing this transmitter system during long-term use.

Regarding alcohol abuse in particular, there are a number of scientific studies implicating norepinephrine in this disorder. In a 2012 paper, I reviewed some of these data, which suggest among other things that alcohol intake is intimately related with the very production of norepinephrine by the body's own biochemical pathways. Alcohol intake, both in animals and in humans, can be modulated by drugs that act on norepinephrine. Pioneers in this field include George Koob at The Scripps Research Institute in California, and William McBride at the Indiana University School of Medicine. An intriguing point is that two drugs, naltrexone and Antabuse, which are commonly used to reduce alcohol intake in humans, may partly achieve their therapeutic effects by acting on norepinephrine signaling.

*   *   *

How might we go about rendering someone exhibiting substance abuse better than well, or at least free from these disorders? The ideas that follow are largely based in theory and require further scientific inquiry to be confirmed.

If the underlying problem principally relates to mental illness, which is fueling the substance abuse, we might treat the problem in the same way we treat other persons with the particular mental illness, as outlined in the various chapters in this book. As mentioned above, certain personality types, such as those high in stimulus seeking traits, may gravitate toward substance abuse. Another personality characteristic that may be associated with substance abuse is dysthymia, which is a fancy term for chronic, mild depression. As I described in my previous book, a large number of individuals may exhibit dysthmia, or a related condition I call "expanded dysthymia", which is an even milder form of chronic depression, and may coexist with other forms of mental illness. If we could treat dysthymia, in all of its varieties, more effectively with psychiatric drugs, we may greatly reduce the number of individuals who abuse substances.

If substance abuse is largely based in elevated norepinephrine signaling, including through its interactions with dopamine transmission, how should we go about preventing or treating it? The same pharmaceutical drug strategies for treating the various mental illnesses in the previous chapters may also be effective here: 1) reduce norepinephrine signaling, 2) raise serotonin and/ or acetylcholine signaling, 3) wait longer than several months to let these pharmaceutical treatments reach maximum therapeutic effect.

To reduce norepinephrine signaling, we can use drugs that lower its synaptic level (clonidine, guanfacine), block alpha receptors (prazosin), or block beta receptors (propranolol). To raise serotonin we can use SSRIs such as Prozac and Zoloft, and to raise acetylcholine signaling we can use cholinesterase inhibitors such as donepezil and galantamine. Raising serotonin or acetylcholine may help treat substance abuse partly because these transmitters may counteract elevated norepinephrine signaling in the brain, and may be most effective when combined with a second drug that lowers norepinephrine signaling. Finally, all of these drugs may take a very long time, such as several years, to reach maximum therapeutic effect, so patience may be required for getting the most out of them.

CHAPTER 11

ADHD, Ritalin, and cognitive enhancement

Attention deficit hyperactivity disorder, often abbreviated as ADHD or ADD, is characterized by an inability to maintain one's focus on something of interest for an extended period of time. Persons with this disorder also often exhibit hyperactivity, including an inability to sit still for very long, especially in the case of children with ADHD. The brain basis of the disorder remains the subject of intensive scientific study, with much of the data implicating so-called hypofrontality, or underfunctioning of the prefrontal cortex. This makes sense, partly because children tend to have weaker prefrontal activation than adults, and ADHD often first emerges in childhood and may become less severe as the child grows older. Psychiatrist and popular author, Daniel Amen, has suggested that there are multiple categories of ADHD that can be revealed through brain imaging techniques, and may in part involve prefrontal deficits.

A more nuanced view of ADHD may extend beyond just the prefrontal cortex, encompassing the very brain circuits that are implicated in our ability, and that of animals, to pay attention to things. These circuits include prefrontal cortex, but also include a region on the side of the brain that is further toward the back, called the posterior parietal cortex. The work of neuroscientists such as Christos Constantinidis at Wake Forest University, and the late Patricia Goldman-Rakic from Yale University, suggests that the posterior parietal cortex and prefrontal cortex work together to allow us to focus on things, while also affecting our ability to form short-term memories. These two brain regions not only may work in tandem, but they are also physically connected to one another through long-range neuronal "wiring". A recent study has suggested that intelligence itself may be related to how well disparate regions of the brain work together: a neural connectedness theory.

Ritalin is probably the most well-known drug that is used to treat ADHD, and it may produce improvement in focus by boosting synaptic dopamine, particularly in prefrontal cortex. (Adderall is another popular ADHD drug, which is basically a cocktail of types of amphetamine molecules, that may produce its principal effect by releasing dopamine into the synapse.) In this regard, Ritalin may be related to the street drug cocaine, which also boosts dopamine in the brain. In some ways, Ritalin has become a "drug of abuse" somewhat like cocaine, as college students and other folks have been taking it (and in some cases, cocaine), especially in recent years, to boost mental functioning. So does Ritalin make people smarter? In some ways, maybe it does, especially in terms of allowing some individuals who use it to take in more information, and then stay on task more effectively in using that information. But this might be a loose definition of intelligence, and maybe is more so a form of temporary performance or cognitive enhancement.

As mentioned above, intelligence may be largely "hardwired" in the brain in terms of neural connectedness, but it may to some degree be modulated by drugs. Mental illnesses, such as bipolar disorder and unipolar depression, which probably involve changes in dopamine and norepinephrine signaling, certainly can affect the rate and subject matter of a person's thoughts, while also modulating his ability to pay attention to things. So I don't think implementing pharmaceutical treatments, such as those that may produce better than well outcomes, will turn ours into a society of Einsteins, but these treatments may induce subtle improvements in cognition, including enhancement of prefrontal "executive" functions. I have little interest in trying to make people smarter through use of drugs, but many folks may likewise have little interest in trying to improve people's moods. Cognition and mood may be linked neurochemically anyway, suggesting that we cannot change one without affecting the other.

Strattera, a drug that in recent years was added to the repertoire of treatments for ADHD, may primarily work by boosting brain norepinephrine, although there is some evidence that it also boosts prefrontal dopamine. The success of this drug in treating at least some cases of ADHD may run counter to my own published ideas suggesting: 1) norepinephrine *deactivates* prefrontal cortex, and 2) norepinephrine tends to activate the left brain hemisphere more so than the right, where the right hemisphere is thought to play a greater role in attentional processing than the left. Something might be missing here, but one possibility that may reconcile these apparent discrepancies is that norepinephrine may activate particular aspects of attention, including our ability to flexibly switch from one item of interest to the next. The ideas of two pioneering researchers mentioned earlier, Amy Arnsten and Trevor Robbins, strongly implicate norepinephrine and dopamine (and possibly other transmitters) in our ability, and that of animals, to pay attention to things that are of interest.

* * *

How might we go about rendering persons with ADHD better than well? The ideas that follow are largely based in theory and require further scientific inquiry to be confirmed. Might we use the same strategies for ADHD as described in the previous chapters for improving mental health in other disorders: lowering norepinephrine signaling, raising serotonin and/or acetylcholine signaling, and waiting longer than a few months for these drugs to reach maximum effect? I think to some degree, if future studies find them effective and safe, we can use these same principles, with some caveats. Unfortunately, with the currently limited state of knowledge regarding ADHD, we may be faced with a "try it, and see what happens" strategy for treating this disorder, which in fact is similar to the uncertainty we still face in treating *all* mental disorders.

As stated above, the relatively new drug Strattera raises brain norepinephrine levels and appears to be effective in treating some persons with ADHD. Here I am suggesting that *lowering* norepinephrine signaling—through drugs such as clonidine, guanfacine, propranolol, prazosin—may also be helpful in some cases. My reasoning is that there is evidence that lowering norepinephrine may increase activation of the prefrontal cortex, also activation of much of the right brain hemisphere, and perhaps particularly the right prefrontal cortex. Such modulation of brain properties may increase a person's ability to pay attention, and also through interactions with prefrontal cortex, reduce his hyperactivity.

Raising serotonin with SSRIs such as Prozac and Zoloft, or boosting acetylcholine with cholinesterase inhibitors (such as donepezil and galantamine) may produce similar effects to lowering norepinephrine signaling. Combining reduction of norepinephrine with boosting of serotonin or acetylcholine may enhance the overall effect of the two separate treatments. Finally, waiting more than a few months to allow these drug treatments to kick in fully may enhance their effects. It is interesting to note that Ritalin and related drugs which act on dopamine kick in within *seconds or minutes* of taking them, depending on how they are taken, but the serotonin, norepinephrine, and acetylcholine drug treatments I am suggesting have much slower, longer lasting effects, which may be a good thing for the person taking them.

CHAPTER 12

PTSD, trauma, and stress

A prominent story in the news as of late, perhaps particularly in the United States, involves soldiers returning from the wars in Iraq and Afghanistan with post-traumatic stress disorder, or PTSD for short. PTSD is a mental disorder that, as the name suggests, can result from exposure to trauma or marked psychological stress, and involves nightmares and flashbacks related to the trauma. It often coexists with major depression and other mental illnesses. Not only is the quality of life for many war veterans greatly reduced by PTSD, but they are also exhibiting a very high suicide rate as a group. The situation has basically spiraled into a crisis, so improved treatments for PTSD are greatly needed as quickly as possible.

Exposure to marked psychological stress or trauma may be a causative factor in many different types of mental illness, but perhaps it is most closely associated with PTSD. The general level of stress that people experience may have been increasing throughout the world in the past several decades, as society is evolving through relatively speedy and prominent changes such as increases in exposure to various technologies, emergence of the Internet and the resulting heightened access to information, the growing world population and to some degree its diminishing resources. James Gleick, author of the classic pop science book, *Chaos*, remarked on some of these changes in another timely book of his, *Faster: The Acceleration of Just About Everything*.

Mental illness rates—at least those based on *diagnosed* cases rather than estimates—appear to be increasing in the past several decades, which is consistent with the possibility that exposure to various stressors has also been ramping upward. Perhaps an increased baseline exposure to stress, accumulated over a lifetime of experiences, makes today's war veterans more likely to develop PTSD after witnessing traumatic events on the battlefield.

In the search for better treatments of PTSD in humans, basic scientists such as myself have been modeling aspects of the illness in mice and rats. These so-called fear conditioning studies—led by such researchers as Joseph LeDoux, Stephen Maren, Michael Fanselow, Mark Bouton, James McGaugh, Michael Davis, Cyril Herry, and Greg Quirk—typically involve exposing the animal to very mild trauma: a slight footshock. Much like Pavlov's dogs that associated hearing a bell ring with getting fed their dinner, the mice or rats in these experiments are often trained to associate hearing a specific sound with getting a shock, since the sound is played around the same time as the shock. Upon receiving these pairings of sound with shock, the animal learns to fear the sound itself, as well as the context (that is, the physical surroundings) of the behavioral box in which he has been placed during the experiment.

In a typical, subsequent "extinction" experiment, the sound is played repeatedly to the animal without administering a shock, and the mouse or rat learns that the sound no longer predicts the shock, and usually shows fewer signs of fear by moving around in the box more instead of freezing (that is, becoming motionless as a sign of fear). Thus, the animal's fear-related behavior has been "extinguished", at least in that physical context, as the animal has learned that the sound apparently no longer predicts the shock. One connection between these rodent experiments and PTSD in humans is that persons with this disorder exhibit impaired extinction, in that they have trouble recognizing that cues which once predicted trauma (such as the sound of explosions on the battlefield) in Iraq or Afghanistan, no longer do (such as the sound of fireworks on the 4th of July) back in their hometown in the United States.

Scientists such as myself can use the fear conditioning experiments to study, for example, the effects of psychiatric drugs on extinction with hopes of developing better treatments for people with PTSD. The existing data suggest that drugs which act on serotonin or norepinephrine, for example, can modulate the ability of mice and rats to extinguish their fear. One issue that has not been studied yet in great detail in animal models of fear is whether long-term treatment with serotonin or norepinephrine altering drugs *prior to* exposure to footshock trauma, versus administration of these drugs *after* exposure to trauma, provides more protection against the effects of this trauma. An area of active research among fear scientists involves identifying the precise brain circuitry that regulates fear. One region of high importance appears to be the amygdala, a roughly almond-shaped region buried deeply in both sides of the brain, which is important in learning fear-related information and for the production of fear-related responses such as freezing (that is, not moving due to fear while monitoring one's surroundings). Another region of high importance in fear regulation is the medial prefrontal cortex, and a third is the hippocampus, which may help store contextual information and is related to memory formation in general.

* * *

How might we render someone with PTSD well, if not better than well? Not surprisingly, the neurotransmitter norepinephrine is already perhaps the signaling molecule most directly implicated in PTSD, partly because it is released in the brain and the rest of the body in response to psychological stress. Serotonin has also received a lot of attention with regard to PTSD.

The ideas that follow are largely based in theory and require further scientific inquiry to be confirmed. A critical point that was raised above concerns treatment strategies for preventing (or minimizing) PTSD in the first place, versus treating it once it has developed. It is unclear whether the military would be interested in pre-emptively placing soldiers on long-term psychiatric drug treatment (such as SSRIs) both before and during exposure to combat, if future research suggests this would be helpful in preventing PTSD. Once PTSD has emerged in a given person, both pharmacological and talk/behavioral therapy treatments are often used, where the latter often consists of so-called exposure therapy that presents the individual with the cues or subject matter that were previously associated with trauma and he learns that he is nonetheless now safe. Exposure therapy can be combined with pharmaceutical treatments, such as antidepressants, where the timing of both types of treatments may be very important, and this is all an area of active research.

Regarding taking pharmaceutical steps to minimize the emergence of PTSD in the first place: I return to a recurring theme in this book, that many if not most people have genetically elevated norepinephrine signaling, which can be made worse by exposure to trauma or marked psychological stress. Norepinephrine may play a general role in the formation of memories, including traumatic ones, suggesting that long-term use of norepinephrine reducing drugs may buffer against the emergence of PTSD in the first place, even if the person is then exposed to trauma. Likewise, taking serotonin or acetylcholine boosting drugs long-term may also provide a buffer against developing PTSD in the first place. Perhaps paradoxically, once PTSD has developed in a given person, these same treatment methods may help minimize the problem, including by putting the brakes on intrusive memories and possibly by improving mood.

The same drug treatment strategies, as described above for other mental illnesses, may be useful in PTSD: 1) lowering norepinephrine signaling, 2) raising serotonin or acetylcholine signaling, 3) waiting longer than just a month or two to let these drugs reach maximum effect. This is not to suggest that exposure therapy, and other forms of psychotherapy, may not be very helpful in treating PTSD. Drugs that enter the brain and reduce norepinephrine signaling include clonidine, guanfacine, propranolol, and prazosin, where this last drug has already been widely used to treat PTSD. Drugs that raise serotonin signaling include the various SSRIs (Prozac, Zoloft, Paxil, Lexapro, Luvox), and those that increase acetylcholine signaling include the cholinesterase inhibitors (donepezil, galantamine, and others). Combining strategies 1 and 2 with a pair of drugs may be more effective than either strategy alone. Finally, I think all of these drugs take longer than a month or two to reach maximum effect in humans, and may require as long as several years.

CHAPTER 13

The "worried well", neuroticism, and expanded dysthymia

Can people who are essentially "normal" be rendered better than well through use of existing psychiatric drugs, such as the SSRIs and other antidepressants? This issue, which was brought up earlier in this book, is of critical importance to the ideas described here. Peter Kramer suggested that so-called normals could have their behavior and to some degree their personality modified by Prozac and related drugs; the case study of his client, Julia, described earlier would also imply that an essentially normal person can be transformed to a significant degree by Prozac. The continuum theory of mental illness, wherein everyone exists somewhere on a range between very healthy and very sick with no sharp cut-off points or categories distinguishing "normal" from "abnormal", suggests that many people may have their mental health improved with pharmaceutical intervention.

The very high worldwide lifetime incidence of mental illness, which has been estimated at roughly fifty percent of the population in some studies, could suggest that many of us are "not far away from mental illness" to begin with. This large group may include many of us among the so-called "worried well" or the neurotic, if you're a fan of Woody Allen or Freud. Evolutionary arguments, made in such books as *Kluge* and *The Accidental Mind*, also suggest that the brain is not a fine-tuned organ, and that shifting it a bit with a drug may improve its performance, including people's mental health. Psychiatrist Michael Norden has suggested that many people share a brain deficiency in serotonin. Genetically high norepinephrine signaling may also have evolved in humans as a means for making us more industrious and productive in our early to middle years, with potentially negative consequences on our long-term health, including emergence of mental illness.

Even if a large fraction of the population who are essentially normal would experience higher quality of life if their brain chemistry was optimized with psychiatric drugs, I am not suggesting, for a variety of reasons, that these persons should do so. I am merely stating that psychiatric drugs may have unexpected transformative powers for a large number of people. I coined the term "expanded dysthymia" in my previous book, *Adjust Your Brain*, to describe a large portion of the population who primarily have no psychiatric diagnosis but could nonetheless be rendered better than well by drug treatment. I drew an analogy between expanded dysthymia and blurry vision, where the former might be corrected by pharmaceutical "eyeglasses" or "contact lenses". Author Stephen Braun independently used the same analogy in his book, *The Science of Happiness*, before I did. John Ratey and Catherine Johnson, in their excellent book, *Shadow Syndromes*, suggest that mild mental illness is indeed very common. It is my hope that thinking of mild to severe mental illness in terms such as blurry vision for the brain may reduce the stigma associated with using psychiatric drugs.

Peter Kramer has made the paradoxical observation that high achievers may in many cases be in the shadow of mental illness in general and depression in particular, and that they may have achieved success partly because they are pathologically "driven". I agree with this assertion, even though we may have instead expected to find a high degree of mental health in people who are successful, and a high level of mental health may in fact accompany success in many cases. Consistent with some degree of mental pathology among many of our highest achievers, it's been suggested that mild depression is the "CEO disease" in corporate America.

Perhaps mild depression or other types of mild mental illness produce dissatisfaction in the individual, driving her to seek higher forms of achievement. I would say that the philosophical concept of nihilism, which suggests that life is essentially meaningless, may have its origins in persons experiencing expanded dysthymia, who to some degree may lack positive perceptual and emotional responses to things in their life.

Psychologist Paul Ekman has made a very successful career of studying how emotions we are experiencing manifest themselves in our facial expressions. His work includes description of so-called microexpressions, which are subtle, involuntary facial expressions that may indicate we are fleetingly experiencing (or concealing) particular emotions. I would like to draw an analogy with this concept, by suggesting that most people experience "microemotions" throughout the day, which are subtle reactions to events, thoughts, or memories that influence our behavior but of which we are barely aware (and may not manifest in subtle facial expressions). I would suggest that without microemotions, which may be disturbed by mild to severe mental illness or improper use of psychiatric drugs, we are profoundly disturbed. In order to function in the long-term and especially to be content, we need to have positive emotional responses that reinforce our behavior throughout the day. As neuroscientist Antonio Damasio has suggested that emotion and cognition may be linked, perhaps without microemotions our ability to reason and reach decisions would be greatly impaired. Perhaps microemotions are slightly impaired in expanded dysthymia, and correcting the condition with psychiatric drugs would not only improve mood and outlook, but also improve cognition.

Peter Kramer has suggested that Prozac can, in some cases at least, quickly transform a wallflower into a social butterfly. Perhaps part of the way this drug achieves such an effect is by enhancing positive emotions. An important part of interacting in an enjoyable manner with others is by sharing positive emotion, including through facial expressions and laughter. If Prozac can enhance positive emotion, perhaps this is how it allows for more positively reinforcing social interaction. On the other hand, serotonin (the molecule that Prozac boosts) has been associated with production of negative emotion in some scientific studies.

Is negative emotion, the apparent flipside of positive experiences, even a bad thing? Maybe too much is. As Peter Kramer has suggested, once a "new" psychological phenomenon or malady is described or popularized, suddenly it seems to be everywhere. Negative emotion may be an example of this. Another, possibly related example is "seriousness", which may also be related to mild depression or compulsiveness, according to Kramer's case studies described earlier. His notion of "cosmetic psychopharmacology" may suggest that Americans want to medicate away negative emotion, for better or worse.

*   *   *

If many people do exhibit expanded dysthymia, a condition of seemingly subtly impaired mental health, can they really be rendered better than well by existing psychiatric drugs? If so, to what degree and in what manner? Popular science author Stephen Braun, in his book *The Science of Happiness*, wrote about his attempts to correct his own minor mood "astigmatism" through use of antidepressants and Ritalin, revealing some of the remarkable effects these drugs had on his behavior and outlook, which I paraphrase now.

Stephen had tinkered with sleep, diet, exercise, alcohol, and caffeine intake over the years, but he inevitably found himself in a sour mood much of the time. He felt that he suffered from some variant of mild depression, possibly too mild to even classify with the clinical term for low-grade depression, "dysthymia". After becoming frustrated for yet again failing to adequately regulate his mood with the "clumsy" drugs known as alcohol and caffeine, and then letting them wash out of his system for months, he found himself in an unpleasant frame of mind. So Stephen sought treatment from a psychiatrist to correct his mood "blurry vision" with an antidepressant or related medication, and the doctor suggested that he may indeed be suffering from a case of dysthymia.

The doctor recommended Prozac, but Stephen vetoed this suggestion since he had heard that drugs such as Prozac can produce sexual side effects. Instead, he received a prescription for Wellbutrin, an antidepressant drug which, unlike Prozac, may not work by boosting the neurotransmitter serotonin. Soon after starting Wellbutrin, Stephen felt, to his surprise, that he had begun paying excessive attention to women's bodies, which he attributed to a slightly enhanced libido. Soon after that, he lost interest in consuming his formerly cherished beverages that contained caffeine or alcohol. But he felt no improvement in mood or energy, even after subsequent increases in dose.

With this setback, Stephen's psychiatrist suggested that maybe he wasn't dysthymic, but rather was just low in energy, and suggested the dopamine boosting drug, Ritalin. The doctor wrote a prescription, but unfortunately Ritalin only produced a slight "buzz" and even made Stephen sleepy at higher doses. With this second setback, the doctor returned to his original suggestion to try Prozac, since it tends to be an "energizing" drug and its sexual side effects tend to be quite mild. Stephen was willing to give it a try.

After about six weeks on Prozac, Stephen noticed that he had been in a good mood as of late, with an improved sense of humor and lower level of perceived stress, with no accompanying sexual side effects. It was a subtle improvement, though. After he spent some more time on Prozac, Stephen decided to let the drug wash out of his system over a number of weeks, to see if the drug was really doing much after all. As it washed away, he did indeed notice a difference, including a return of his natural tenseness and nervousness, and even cynicism and self-righteousness.

Stephen then returned to his psychiatrist and left with a prescription for another SSRI, Celexa (which is very similar in molecular structure to the drug, Lexapro). This drug generated a similar, subtle improvement in his mood to that produced by Prozac. At the time of his writing, Stephen thought he might take Celexa on a long-term basis, as he felt it may indeed be ameliorating his mood "astigmatism".

The above case study may suggest that existing psychiatric drugs have subtle, albeit significant effects in persons such as Stephen who fall within the range of "normal". One point that he makes, which I would like to emphasize, is that the future of psychopharmacology really does lie in use of drugs that have subtle effects, in as much as one doesn't feel "drugged" while on them, unlike with drugs of abuse like alcohol or cocaine that have essentially immediate, obvious effects. A drug (such as Prozac) that quietly does its job in improving quality of life represents the future of psychopharmacology, and benzodiazepines (such as Xanax and Valium) and barbiturates represent the past. The therapeutic effects of these so-called subtle drugs may not actually be so subtle if they were used properly, such as giving them enough time to reach maximum effect. Another point to note from this case study is the trial-and-error nature of modern psychiatric drug treatment: a try this, try that approach that is still unfortunately the way a given person is typically treated.

How might we render someone in the shadow of mental illness better than well, if the individual is inclined to seek treatment? The ideas that follow are largely based in theory and require further scientific inquiry to be confirmed.

In keeping with a recurring theme in this book (and in my previous one, *Adjust Your Brain*), I think that most people, mainly through genetics, have reduced serotonin signaling and/or enhanced norepinephrine signaling. This includes most people with moderate to severe mental illness, as well as those with expanded dysthymia. A small minority of persons, with or without mental illness, have elevated serotonin signaling and/or reduced norepinephrine signaling. So for most people who might want to try improving their mental health with psychiatric drugs, the same strategy described above for various mental illnesses may apply: 1) lower norepinephrine signaling (with clonidine, guanfacine, propranolol, or prazosin), 2) raise serotonin (with

Prozac, Zoloft, Paxil, Lexapro, Luvox) or acetylcholine signaling (with cholinesterase inhibitors such as donepezil, galantamine, and others), 3) wait more than a few months to allow these drugs to reach maximum effect. Combining strategies 1 and 2 with a pair of drugs may produce an interaction that improves the effect of either drug alone.

CHAPTER 14

Better than well for the body

As science goes, the early 20th century may have been the era of theoretical physics, when Einstein, Heisenberg, Dirac, and their many ingenious colleagues were making great strides for that field. I would say that the early 21st century is the era of biomedical research, or simply the "Era of Disease". The field of medical research may now be on the cusp of making great breakthroughs in how to prevent or treat many of the major (as well as the less common) diseases of the body, such as Alzheimer's disease and various types of cancer, partly by developing a greater understanding of their mechanistic processes.

Much of disease research has focused on molecular processes that take place inside cells. Cancer and to some degree Alzheimer's disease are two prominent examples of the intracellular (that is, inside of cells) molecular focus of inquiry by scientists. In my own published work, I have suggested that the extracellular (that is, outside of cells) signaling molecule and neurotransmitter, norepinephrine, plays a very prominent role in many of the major diseases of the body, and possibly in many of the less common ones too. Norepinephrine is not just a signaling molecule in the brain, but also interacts with nearly every (if not every) organ of the body, and the series of nerves that spray it onto these organs is part of the so-called sympathetic nervous system.

One of the functions of the sympathetic nervous system is mediating the so-called fight-or-flight response to immediate dangers or stressors: if you see a bear in the woods, this system releases norepinephrine and other "stress hormones", which for example make your heart beat faster and divert blood flow to your muscles, so you can run away more effectively. The sympathetic nervous system is functionally opposed by the parasympathetic nervous system, which uses acetylcholine as its output molecule, and enhances our ability to "rest and digest". The sympathetic and parasympathetic nervous systems, which can be thought of as sort of a yin and yang for the body, are two branches of what's called the autonomic nervous system.

The conventional wisdom is that healthy people have an essentially normal autonomic nervous system, but I instead have suggested in various scientific publications that many if not most people have genetically elevated sympathetic output and relatively diminished parasympathetic drive. One can make various evolutionary (and other) arguments as to why this may be the case. Regardless of its origins, such an autonomic nervous system imbalance could lead to the body engaging in insufficient rest and digest "maintenance" processes, resulting in the emergence of a number of diseases. I have suggested that this list includes: cancer, Alzheimer's disease, epilepsy, asthma, diabetes, arthritis, glaucoma, macular degeneration, lupus, atrial fibrillation, high blood pressure, obesity, and metabolic syndrome. I'm not suggesting that elevated norepinephrine is the *only* factor in these diseases, just that it may be an important one. Consistent with this theory, a number of recent studies have shown that beta blocker drugs (which, as you'll recall, block a type of norepinephrine receptor) may help prevent or treat some types of cancer.

Type I diabetes and lupus are considered to be autoimmune disorders, where the body's immune system attacks its own tissues. One possibility is that elevated norepinephrine signaling affects a wide range of autoimmune disorders, including these two diseases and multiple sclerosis, Sjogren's syndrome, Crohn's disease, and others. As to *how* elevated norepinephrine may help cause these autoimmune diseases and the other diseases listed above: it may do so by interacting with molecular pathways inside of cells that are already implicated in diseases in these various organs, including modulation of the immune system and inflammatory processes.

In his book, *Better than Well: American Medicine Meets the American Dream*, academic researcher Carl Elliot suggests that Americans are very interested in modifying their bodies through various procedures, such as plastic surgery, although he isn't referring to the list of diseases I just described. Can we use various existing drugs, such as those that reduce norepinephrine signaling, to help prevent or treat a wide range of diseases through "pharmacological modification"? Aspirin may be one such "generalist" drug for treating many diseases, including various types of cancer, although it doesn't act directly on norepinephrine signaling (but may do so indirectly, through some of its molecular effects).

The norepinephrine transmission lowering drugs may prove to be even more powerful and general in this role than aspirin, by preventing or treating an even wider array of diseases, including but not limited to psychiatric and neurological ailments. Norepinephrine reducing drugs may be a shield or "firewall" against a variety of diseases, for a large number of individuals, and perhaps this effect would be enhanced by boosting acetylcholine signaling with cholinesterase inhibitors. The psychiatric drugs we have been discussing do not just penetrate the brain, but are dispersed throughout the body and could thereby directly affect various disease processes. They may also indirectly affect diseases outside of the brain by having effects on the brain's regulation of the autonomic nervous system. These drugs could be combined with more narrowly targeted therapies, including more targeted drugs, for a given disease including certain types of cancer. On the other hand, some people probably have genetically *diminished* norepinephrine signaling, where taking norepinephrine lowering drugs on a long-term basis may be harmful, psychologically and in its consequences for the above various diseases.

CHAPTER 15

Sociopathy, psychoticism, and creativity

Hans Eysenck, the late and highly accomplished psychologist, helped put forth a controversial personality model decades ago that was based in three elements: psychoticism, extraversion, and neuroticism (P-E-N, for short), suggesting that variation in these characteristics may largely explain the diversity of human behavior. This model is still very much of interest today, since psychoticism may be closely related to a timely topic in the field of psychology, that of psychopathy or sociopathy. Popular books such as *The Sociopath Next Door* and *Confessions of a Sociopath* have received a good deal of attention among the general public as of late.

Eysenck suggested that psychoticism is characterized by hostility and aggression toward others, may also be related to mental disorders such as schizophrenia, and may run in families in which schizophrenia exists. Intriguingly, according to Eysenck a high degree of psychoticism may be correlated with high levels of creativity, and even outright genius, when mated with a high degree of intelligence in the individual. This assertion is consistent with the colloquial notion that "madness" and genius are related phenomena.

It has also been suggested that psychoticism and schizophrenia are related to elevated levels of dopamine signaling in the brain. Outright schizophrenia produces a degree of brain dysfunction that is so profound as to stifle a number of healthy mental processes including creativity. On the other hand, schizotypy, which may be a milder variant of full-blown schizophrenia, is associated with above average levels of creativity. Also, unaffected family members of persons with these mental disorders exhibit above average levels of creativity.

Eminent author and psychiatric researcher Kay Jamison has suggested that bipolar disorder, which may in part involve cycling levels of brain dopamine, is also associated with above average creativity. Consistent with this idea, Jamison has found in her research that bipolar disorder is more commonly found among artists, such as fiction writers and poets, than it is in the general population, and outlined these ideas in her classic book, *Touched with Fire*. I agree with Jamison's conclusions, and in my previous book I suggested that bipolar disorder being more common among artists is actually a special case of a more general phenomenon: all or nearly all artists have elevated brain norepinephrine signaling, including those with bipolar disorder. In this scenario, many artists may also have elevated dopamine signaling. Why might elevated norepinephrine signaling help make someone an artist? The effect could be produced by this transmitter helping to activate the left hemisphere of the brain and thereby enhancing a sense of aesthetics. Dopamine may interact with norepinephrine in enhancing the flow of ideas and increasing mental flexibility, thereby boosting creativity.

Duke University neuroscientist Miguel Nicolelis and co-workers have suggested that elevated dopaminergic signaling may produce a superimposition of the sleeping mind on the waking one (to frame this in Freudian terms, as they did in one of their publications), in that awake and active mice with enhanced dopamine activity in response to novel stimuli show brain activity patterns similar to those found while we are dreaming. Perhaps this observation is related to the psychiatric phenomenon of depersonalization, wherein persons with depression or other disorders have a feeling of "walking in a dream" while completely awake.

In scientific studies, sociopathy is often associated with reduced serotonin signaling, which may interfere with the functioning of prefrontal cortex, producing impulsivity and perhaps other traits associated with sociopathy, such as lack of conscience and remorse. In this view, prefrontal dysfunction plays a key role in making a sociopath a sociopath. An alternative theory, that I would suggest, is that some sociopaths have *enhanced* prefrontal functioning, producing deviousness and perhaps even blatant dishonesty. To summarize, sociopathy, psychoticism, and creativity are obviously not the same thing but may have overlapping properties, and may be present to some degree in the same person.

CHAPTER 16

Dominance and eminence

We can think of social dominance, as in the "alpha" male or female in certain species of animals that live in groups with pecking orders, as being at least coarsely related to social interaction in humans. One of the scientific studies I referred to earlier suggested that a serotonin boosting antidepressant can modulate assertiveness and even degree of eye contact among people sharing an apartment. This nearly humorous observation suggests that serotonin plays a role in social dominance, a view that has indeed been supported by a number of human and animal studies, many of which assert that boosting serotonin increases social dominance. However, conflicting findings have been reported.

The relatively large scientific literature on social dominance, where many of these studies have been performed in animals, also suggests that high levels of norepinephrine and dopamine can be associated with being the "alpha". Some of these studies may imply that genetic or at least long-standing levels of these transmitters help produce dominance, whereas others emphasize that the levels (at least in some animal species) can shift when the individual achieves a dominant position in the group. So, do our leaders in present-day society have elevated levels of monoamines, either before or after they become leaders? It seems like almost a comical issue to raise in humans, as we might think there's a lot more to leadership, prominence, and success than our neurotransmitter systems, which is probably true. For example, what about general intelligence, social skills, and common sense, not to mention physical attributes? But I would suggest that, perhaps paradoxically, many people who do rise to prominence may indeed have elevated monoamine signaling, which could be related to aggressiveness or assertiveness, and even to outright hypomania, as in John Gartner's book, *The Hypomanic Edge*.

A somewhat different theory on how the monoamines may help produce dominance is that they do so most effectively when at mid-range values. In other words, too much or too little actually detracts from dominance. This idea may dovetail with the observation that boosting serotonin tends to promote dominance, because most people, as I've stated throughout this book, tend to have low serotonin transmission. In this scenario, having mid-range serotonin and norepinephrine transmission may decrease depression and many other mental disorders, while producing dominant personality characteristics. Perhaps this psychological effect is accompanied by making the individual less inclined to help others and more inclined to help himself. He's no longer part of the supporting cast but has become the star of the show, for better or worse. However, helping others may be another means for achieving and maintaining power. Having mid-range values of the monoamines may also increase stress tolerance, which could be a critical aspect of being an alpha, because it's stressful at the top. If someone is given an antidepressant drug, such that she is able to tolerate stress more easily and rise to a position of prominence as a result, is she better than well?

A related topic to that of social dominance is eminence, which may be by definition a uniquely human measure. Eminence is indicated by how prominent someone becomes in society, including in various fields of endeavor such as business, the military, science, athletics, and the arts. In his comprehensive book, *The Price of Greatness*, psychiatric researcher Arnold Ludwig analyzed biographical information from one thousand prominent persons who lived in the twentieth century. Two conclusions Ludwig reached regarding the persons on his list who achieved the highest levels of eminence: they tended to be loners and they also exhibited contrarianism, which is a tendency to go against the grain. In other words, they were reclusive mavericks. My suggestion here is that both of these characteristics—reclusiveness and contrarianism—may be the result of genetically elevated activation of prefrontal cortex. I think this is the brain basis of many, but certainly not all, cases of eminence. In this scenario, the vast majority of persons in the population do not exhibit excessive prefrontal activation, which could be partly related to most people being weak in serotonin signaling and strong in norepinephrine transmission. The flipside of contrarianism may be clannishness—a tendency to form groups, to the exclusion of "outsiders"—which is far more common and may be related to low prefrontal activation, or low activation of particular prefrontal subregions through enhanced norepinephrine signaling.

A few more points on eminence and the prefrontal cortex. In *Listening to Prozac*, Peter Kramer discusses the so-called "aloneness effect", which simply relates to some if not most people (or animals) really not enjoying being alone. Kramer describes research suggesting that this phenomenon is causally related to low serotonin signaling. If so, perhaps this putative effect of serotonin relates to the more general phenomenon of activation of prefrontal cortex by serotonin, dopamine, genetics, and perhaps other inputs. Perhaps how one produces the "eccentric billionaire" personality type, for example, is through excessive activation of prefrontal cortex via these factors, possibly leading to someone who is reclusive, among other traits caused by such activation. One possibility is that either very high or very low levels of prefrontal activation produce "madness", which could be partially related to eccentricity. A final note on this topic: molecular biologist and author Samuel Barondes has noted findings suggesting that eminence runs in families and may therefore have, at least partially, a genetic basis.

CHAPTER 17

Different from well

A principal focus of this book has been to put forth the idea that some persons can be rendered better than well through proper use of existing psychiatric drugs, as suggested by Peter Kramer over twenty years ago. This is certainly a controversial assertion that has been and continues to be viewed with a great deal of skepticism, as it probably should be, especially if we suggest that a large fraction of the population can be rendered better off. It is a work in progress, for current and future generations of scientists and mental health professionals to unravel in a clearer fashion.

As stated earlier, a somewhat less controversial claim at this point may be that persons can be rendered "different from well" by existing psychiatric drugs, such as Prozac. This means that psychiatric drugs are capable not only of helping people recover from mental illness, but may also transform them to some degree, personality-wise and behaviorally, in the process, while not necessarily leaving them "better off". A related idea is that so-called normal people can be transformed by these drugs, as in the example of Stephen Braun's case study described above (although it could be argued that he was suffering from dysthymia). Examples of psychiatric drugs producing different from well outcomes include antidepressants affecting social dominance in persons (and animals), as well as antidepressants worsening mood cycling in persons with bipolar disorder.

This last point about bipolar disorder brings up the notion of "worse than well" outcomes of taking a psychiatric drug, where I don't mean the usual side effects of a drug, such as dry mouth or nausea. Instead, worse than well here refers to a drug having its intended effect in the brain, such as Prozac boosting serotonin, but for the given person this effect makes them worse off mentally, possibly through subtle personality changes or other means such as mood dysregulation. A recurring theme in this book, and my previous one, is that most people have diminished serotonin signaling and/or elevated norepinephrine signaling, largely through genetics. In such persons, reducing serotonin signaling further or boosting norepinephrine further with a drug, should make them worse than well. Boosting serotonin or lowering norepinephrine, on the other hand, may render such persons better than well. In this scenario, achieving mid-range values for the modulatory neurotransmitters—serotonin, norepinephrine, dopamine, acetylcholine, in particular—either genetically or through use of psychiatric drugs, makes for a more mentally healthy individual, in my opinion.

When a person taking an antidepressant or other psychiatric drug decides for himself whether it is rendering him better than well, or is producing more so a neutral transformation that he would simply call different from well, he may be biased toward calling it better than well due to a novelty effect of the drug. In other words, newer is sometimes better, and having some sort of psychiatric change such as greater assertiveness or increased stress tolerance may bias the person toward thinking he is better off when really he both gained and also lost some positive traits, as in Peter Kramer's client Sam, described in the first chapter. On the other hand, a person may have a negative reaction to novel effects of a drug, dwelling on the perceived negative aspects of the effect without realizing there were positive ones.

Drugs may not only render some people different from well, but also people are of course different from one another to begin with, behaviorally and neurochemically. There may be no such thing as a standard, "normal" person. Just look at the variability in the genetics of the modulatory neurotransmitter systems, including the serotonin reuptake transporter, where the alleles (that is, varieties of gene) differ from person to person and have effects on behavior as well, such as ability to recover from significant stress or trauma.

When examining the genetics of mental health, we must keep in mind that for most of our genes, we have two copies. One possibility is that so-called heterozygotes, who have two different alleles for the given neurotransmitter-related gene, tend to be healthier than persons who have two of the same copies. For example, heterozygotes for the gene that regulates the serotonin transporter may have mid-range values of serotonin transmission, which could render them mentally healthier than persons with two of the same copies, who may have too much or too little serotonin. This sort of reasoning may suggest that some individuals are born worse than well, simply due to the genes they inherited from their parents.

A few more thoughts on the effects of psychiatric drugs—and perhaps antidepressants in particular—on the monoamines, in relation to different from well. Anecdotally, drugs such as Prozac have been reported to produce emotional stabilization, perhaps deadening both highs and lows, in particular individuals. Many people do not find this effect favorable, although it may increase stress tolerance as well as boosting social dominance characteristics. I would suggest that this emotional deadening effect may occur in the first several months on these drugs, whereas perhaps more euphoric effects take place much later. I would also propose that adjusting the modulatory transmitters with drugs to mid-range values produces this delayed outcome, which may be at the heart of greatly delayed better than well effects, where few people remain on the same drug regimen long enough to experience this.

CHAPTER 18

Morality and ethics

Many people may find the idea of administering psychiatric drugs to a sizeable fraction of the population, a large portion of whom are considered essentially normal, to be unethical or immoral. Of course, this is already being done, especially in the United States, where tens of millions of people have taken or continue to take antidepressants, for example. Psychiatrist Peter Breggin, author of passionately argued books such as *Toxic Psychiatry* and *Your Drug May Be Your Problem* (the latter book was co-authored with David Cohen), appears to be against the use of psychiatric drugs in anyone at all. To paraphrase his ideas: drugs may not only be harmful to the body (including the brain), but also giving them to a person is immoral. Breggin, who not surprisingly isn't a fan of the drug companies, thinks that persons with psychiatric disorders should be given moral support by an empathetic doctor, but never (or perhaps almost never) treated with psychiatric drugs. I think this is an extremist position, given the overwhelming evidence that psychiatric drugs can be helpful for a large number of individuals.

However, Breggin does have a point, especially when we consider giving drugs, on a broad scale, to so-called normals. Perhaps implementing better than well treatment in various people would be a frightening scenario, akin to science fiction or the workings of Doctor Frankenstein. It has been suggested that medicating the masses smacks of *Brave New World* for the new millennium, a reference to Aldous Huxley's famous novel where citizens living in a totalitarian regime were medicated into submission by a fictional drug called soma. Of course, the masses in present day society are already being medicated, of their own choice, by Prozac and other SSRIs (as well as various drugs of abuse), and I wouldn't say this is holding anyone in submission. I would argue that better than well is indeed not a frightening or unethical prospect, but simply is a way to allow people to become mentally and physically healthier, leading to higher quality of life.

A recent scientific paper, mentioned in Chapter 2, suggests that boosting serotonin with antidepressants such as SSRIs may enhance moral decision making. Perhaps this effect is mediated by boosting serotonin in the prefrontal cortex, thereby activating this circuitry to a greater degree. As mentioned earlier, the prefrontal cortex and surrounding brain regions may contain so-called mirror neurons that could enhance our sense of empathy. More generally, perhaps rendering people better than well with drugs may make them more ethical in their behavioral patterns, including through enhancement of empathy.

I am certainly willing to entertain arguments to the contrary. What if, for example, activation of prefrontal cortex produces increased deviousness? Or a certain wiliness that it may take to maneuver about and eventually succeed in a dog-eat-dog world? Most of the existing evidence would suggest that *decreased* prefrontal activity is associated with unethical behavior including sociopathy, but the jury is still out on this topic, as is the case for most questions in neuroscience, and science in general. Perhaps in less extreme cases than outright sociopathy, decreased prefrontal activation would simply increase deceptiveness in a given individual. Perhaps this is what helps make a con artist who he or she is.

To shift the topic slightly, perhaps Peter Kramer is correct when he states that the changes produced by drugs such as Prozac can be "cosmetic". Maybe he is less so correct about these drugs truly transforming personality. The effect could be more of a superficial or at least subtle change, an enhancement of one's positive experiences and skillset, which nonetheless leaves the core of the self intact. To me, this is an essential issue to understand in evaluating the ethics of using drugs such as SSRIs. Even if these drugs can truly transform who we are, this would not necessarily make their use immoral, but we would obviously want to investigate this effect in greater detail.

CHAPTER 19

Futurism, society, and general conclusions

What does the prospect of potentially rendering a large portion of the population better than well—or different from well—hold for the future of society, and the world in general? I would suggest that the answer needs to address three issues: 1) how many people would receive such treatment, 2) what is the nature of the changes in the individual, in terms of personality and other factors, 3) and how large is the effect in a given person? A more minor issue may be how quickly psychiatric drugs can produce their effects in a given person. If better than well takes many years to reach maximum effect with existing drugs (and perhaps with all future drugs), the process might become somewhat of a rite of passage for adults who take these medications. My overall impression at this point, which lies in contrast to the conclusions I reached in my previous book, is that even if a large number of persons would experience significantly higher quality of life on these drugs, it may not really have that much of an effect on society. This is an open question, in my opinion.

Futurist Ray Kurzweil, author of the pop science books *The Age of Spiritual Machines* and *The Singularity is Near,* thinks that technology and innovation, including through the development of intelligent machines, may be key to making life better and more interesting down the road. While I don't deny that technology can be a cool thing, I would suggest that better than well may really be what Kurzweil and other futurists have been waiting for, even though they didn't realize it.

To return to the subject of better than well being akin to a *Brave New World* scenario: I would argue that, to a limited degree, we're already living in a brave new world, with widespread violence such as school shootings, war, and totalitarian governments. Perhaps better than well would help undo this. Even capitalism is partly based on defeating someone else; it's somewhat of a zero sum game. Many people aren't willing to wait very long for things in this society, possibly to the detriment of considering the effects on future developments, such as human impact on the environment. People are restless and want immediate gratification—which is part of the way capitalism functions—and this behavior could be related to low prefrontal cortical functioning. If many people were much more patient, that alone may improve society. This idea is related to my earlier argument about better than well producing generalist versus specialized personalities, where the generalist individual is more well-rounded and capable of a greater range of constructive behaviors. If people were more cooperative, empathetic, and patient, perhaps our economic system could be altered in a manner that would benefit nearly everyone.

A potential problem for society may arise if large numbers of people take antidepressants such as Prozac and these drugs really do increase social dominance, as suggested earlier. Not everyone can be the "alpha" in group situations, such as in the workplace, on sports teams, or in political parties. We need a large supporting cast for society to function normally, even though most parents in America seem to want their kids to be leaders and not followers, as if being a follower is a flawed way of operating. As psychiatrist Michael Norden suggested, giving antidepressants to the masses is akin to a giant, uncontrolled experiment, where we really don't fully understand the ramifications and potential outcome.

As we begin to understand potentially better than well treatments in psychiatry, the entire field is improving its treatment methods in the process. Having objective ways, called biomarkers, for monitoring the effects of psychiatric drug treatment may help patients tremendously. One way of doing so is through use of non-invasive brain imaging techniques such as functional magnetic resonance imaging (fMRI) or positron emission tomography (PET). I would suggest that fMRI in particular may play a central role in the psychiatry of the future, at least in difficult to treat individuals. Whether, in the future, nearly *everyone* who is treated with psychiatric drugs has the effects monitored through fMRI, or some superior yet-to-be-invented technology, is an open question. The logistics of scanning millions of people on a regular basis may make doing so not readily feasible, but I think it could be arranged if this approach is helpful enough in treating patients. One brain region of interest that could be monitored by fMRI in depressed persons is area 25, which is the general brain region where Helen Mayberg and colleagues have been providing deep brain stimulation with surgically implanted electrodes, as described earlier. Another critical means for improving psychiatric drug treatment, in my opinion, is to make better use of norepinephrine transmission reducing medications.

What does the future hold for psychiatry in terms of the drugs that will be used most commonly? As Stephen Braun has suggested, a pill that makes people feel "drugged" or intoxicated, like taking alcohol or cocaine, will never, in my opinion, become a long-term solution by society for improving mental health for the masses. Benzodiazepines and barbiturates had their heyday decades ago and I don't think they'll ever make a comeback in great numbers. But, as Samuel Barondes points out, perhaps drugs with similar mechanisms of action to these could be produced that don't cause sedation as a side effect. A common misconception about serotonin or norepinephrine boosting antidepressant drugs, largely propagated by people who have never taken them, is that they are "uppers" or stimulants that make one feel "high". Actually, their effects are a lot more subtle than this, and they do not produce intoxication, hence the fact that they are not abused like street drugs.

If better than well is a real phenomenon, and if it would be implemented in a large fraction of the population to a significant degree, it could be a disruptive discovery or innovation, as they say in the business world: disruptive for psychiatrists and other health care professionals administering these treatments, disruptive for the pharmaceutical industry, and disruptive in terms of how people go about getting treatment for themselves. The overall effect of these potential ramifications is difficult to foresee.

We all want better health for ourselves and those we care about, and we want a better psychiatry. And as for the idealists, and even those who don't count themselves in this group, we want a better world in general. If better than well increases empathy, perhaps it could lead to more cooperative interaction among individuals, and even among individuals who rule nations. The way people now typically behave toward one another, it may suggest that empathy is in short supply.

To summarize my overall thoughts as of this writing: can psychiatric drugs render people different from well? Definitely. Can these drugs make some people better than well? Most likely. But how many people would stand to benefit from these techniques, and to what degree, remains unanswered. These are issues for our generation and future generations of curious individuals to address.

General References

American Psychiatric Association: *Diagnostic and Statistical Manual of Mental Disorders*, Fourth Edition, Text Revision; American Psychiatric Association, Washington, DC, 2000.

Samuel H. Barondes, *Better than Prozac*, Oxford University Press, New York, NY, 2003.

Paul J. Fitzgerald, *Adjust Your Brain*, O Books, Winchester, United Kingdom, 2007.

Frederick K. Goodwin, Kay R. Jamison, *Manic-Depressive Illness*, Oxford University Press, New York, NY, 1990.

Aldous Huxley, *Brave New World*, Harper & Brothers, New York, NY, 1932.

Kay R. Jamison, *Touched with Fire*, Free Press, New York, NY, 1993.

Kay R. Jamison, *An Unquiet Mind*, Knopf, New York, NY, 1995.

Eric R. Kandel, James H. Schwartz, Thomas M. Jessell, *Principles of Neural Science, 4th Edition*, McGraw-Hill Medical, New York, NY, 2000.

Peter D. Kramer, *Against Depression*, Viking Penguin, New York, NY, 2005.

Peter D. Kramer, *Listening to Prozac*, Viking Penguin, New York, NY, 1993.

Paul R. McHugh, Phillip R. Slavney, *The Perspectives of Psychiatry, 2nd Edition*, The Johns Hopkins University Press, Baltimore, MD, 1998.

John Nolte, *The Human Brain*, Mosby-Year Book, St. Louis, Missouri, 1993.

Michael J. Norden, *Beyond Prozac*, ReganBooks, New York, NY, 1995.

John J. Ratey, Catherine Johnson, *Shadow Syndromes*, Bantam Books, New York, NY, 1998.

REFERENCES FOR PARTICULAR CHAPTERS

CHAPTER 1. PETER KRAMER POPULARIZES A CONCEPT

Marcia Angell, *The Truth About the Drug Companies*, Random House, New York, NY, 2005.

Peter R. Breggin, Ginger Ross Breggin, *Talking Back to Prozac*, St. Martin's Press, New York, NY, 1994.

Ronald W. Dworkin, *Artificial Happiness*, Basic Books, New York, NY, 2007.

Gary Greenberg, *Manufacturing Depression*, Simon & Schuster, New York, NY, 2010.

David Healy, *Let them Eat Prozac*, New York University Press, New York, NY, 2006.

Irving Kirsch, *The Emperor's New Drugs*, Basic Books, New York, NY, 2011.

Peter D. Kramer, *Listening to Prozac*, Viking Penguin, New York, NY, 1993.

CHAPTER 2. ZOOMING IN ON BETTER THAN WELL

(Crockett et al. 2010): "For example, a placebo controlled study (which is a study where some people receive drug and others merely receive an inactive pill, and the persons aren't aware of which treatment they were given) in which the SSRI Lexapro was given to healthy persons found that it altered moral judgments. These persons were presented with hypothetical moral dilemmas, where they were asked, for example, if they would allow an innocent person to be killed if it would save five other lives? Enhancing serotonin with Lexapro made the people in the study more likely to judge harmful actions as forbidden, but only for emotionally salient hypothetical harms."

Crockett et al. (2010) Serotonin selectively influences moral judgment and behavior through effects on harm aversion. Proc Natl Acad Sci USA 107:17433-8.

(Tse and Bond 2002): "Another placebo controlled study of Lexapro in healthy persons examined the drug's effect on social interaction with a roommate in an apartment over several weeks, as well as subsequent interaction with a stranger. On drug, the persons were rated as less submissive by their roommates, showed a dominant pattern of eye contact and were more cooperative in interacting with the stranger in a role playing game."

Tse and Bond (2002) Serotonergic intervention affects both social dominance and affiliative behaviour. Psychopharmacology (Berl) 161:324-30.

(Harmer et al. 2003): "A third placebo controlled study of Lexapro, in healthy females, where drug was given transiently in an intravenous manner, found that Lexapro selectively enhanced recognition of facial expressions of fear and happiness, without affecting recognition of other emotions."

Harmer et al. (2003) Acute SSRI administration affects the processing of social cues in healthy volunteers. Neuropsychopharmacology 28:148-52.

(Brody et al. 2000): "A study of Paxil in persons with major depression or obsessive-compulsive disorder found that this drug, while not showing differences in effect between these two groups, reduced the trait of "harm avoidance" (that is, avoiding bad things) in drug responders more so than in non-responders, and on the whole tended to increase social dominance and decrease hostility in social situations in those treated with drug."

Brody et al. (2000) Personality changes in adult subjects with major depressive disorder or obsessive-compulsive disorder treated with paroxetine. J Clin Psychiatry 61:349-55.

(Dunlop et al. 2011): "An intriguing study of persons with major depression measured the effects of Zoloft on psychopathic personality traits. Independent of its effects on depression, Zoloft increased adaptive traits traditionally observed in psychopathic individuals, including social charm and interpersonal and physical boldness. On the other hand Zoloft reduced maladaptive traits associated with psychopathy, including impulsivity (that is, acting on a whim without thinking things through)."

Dunlop et al. (2011) The effects of sertraline on psychopathic traits. Int Clin Psychopharmacol 26:329-37.

Stephen Braun, *The Science of Happiness*, Wiley, Hoboken, NJ, 2000.

Francis S. Collins, *The Language of God*, Free Press, New York, NY, 2006.

Paul J. Fitzgerald, *Adjust Your Brain*, O Books, Winchester, United Kingdom, 2007.

Peter D. Kramer, *Freud: Inventor of the Modern Mind*, HarperCollins, New York, NY, 2006.

David J. Linden, *The Accidental Mind*, Harvard University Press, Cambridge, MA, 2007.

Gary Marcus, *Kluge*, Houghton Mifflin, New York, NY, 2008.

Michael J. Norden, *Beyond Prozac*, William Morrow, New York, NY, 1995.

Lauren Slater, *Prozac Diary*, Random House, New York, NY, 1998.

Elizabeth Wurtzel, *Prozac Nation*, Houghton Mifflin, New York, NY, 1994.

CHAPTER 3. THE CHEMICALS BETWEEN US

Jerrold S. Meyer, Linda F. Quenzer, *Psychopharmacology*, Sinauer, Sunderland, MA 2004.

Paul J. Fitzgerald, Ph.D.

Betram Katzung, Susan Masters, Anthony Trevor, *Basic and Clinical Pharmacology (12ᵗʰ Edition)*, McGraw-Hill Medical, New York, NY, 2011.

(Felleman and Van Essen 1991): "Lending credence to the analogy of generals and foot soldiers for neurotransmitter systems, different brain areas, such as the many that process visual information, appear to have a hierarchical relationship with one another."

Felleman and Van Essen (1991) Distributed hierarchical processing in the primate cerebral cortex. Cereb Cortex 1:1-47.

(Fitzgerald 2011): "Pharmaceutical drugs that enhance either serotonin or norepinephrine signaling can reduce impulsivity (which means acting on a whim without thinking things through)."

Fitzgerald (2011) A neurochemical yin and yang: Does serotonin activate and norepinephrine deactivate the prefrontal cortex? Psychopharmacol (Berl) 213:171-82.

(Fitzgerald 2012): "In contrast, a recent scientific paper I wrote suggests that serotonin and norepinephrine may be opposed to one another in terms of "lateralized" functions of the brain, with serotonin tending to activate the right side of the brain and norepinephrine the left."

Fitzgerald (2012) Whose side are you on: does serotonin preferentially activate the right hemisphere and norepinephrine the left? Med Hypotheses 79:250-4.

(Cloninger 1986): "Regarding potential independence of function between these two transmitters: in the 1980s, eminent psychiatric researcher C. Robert Cloninger suggested that serotonin modulates a behavioral effect called "harm avoidance" that was mentioned above, whereas norepinephrine modulates "reward dependence"."

Cloninger (1986) A unified biosocial theory of personality and its role in the development of anxiety states. Psychiatr Dev 4:167-226.

(Volkow et al. 2013): "A more complex theory is that some, if not all, transmitters straddle the divide between being exclusively inhibitory or solely excitatory; dopamine may be an example of such a "hybrid" transmitter system." (Author's note: this citation relates to the idea of dopamine having inhibitory properties.)

Volkow et al. (2013) Predominance of D2 receptors in mediating dopamine's effects in brain metabolism: effects of alcoholism. J Neurosci 33:4527-35.

(Grace 1991): "Another aspect of neurotransmitter functioning, which has been studied in vivid detail by Anthony Grace and his colleagues at the University of Pittsburgh, is so-called tonic or phasic release."

Grace AA (1991) Phasic versus tonic dopamine release and the modulation of dopamine system responsivity: a hypothesis for the etiology of schizophrenia. Neuroscience 41:1-24.

(Nishizawa et al. 1997): "Another interesting point about serotonin is that brain imaging data suggest men generate about 50% higher brain levels of it than women do."

Nishizawa et al. (1997) Differences between males and females in rates of serotonin synthesis in human brain. Proc Natl Acad Sci USA 94:5308-5313.

CHAPTER 4. NEUROTRANSMITTER IMBALANCE THEORIES AND BEYOND

Schildkraut (1965) The catecholamine hypothesis of affective disorders: a review of supporting evidence. Am J Psychiatry 122:509-522.

Coppen (1967) The biochemistry of affective disorders. Br J Psychiatry 113:1237-1264.

Janowsky et al. (1972) A cholinergic-adrenergic hypothesis of mania and depression. Lancet 2:632-635.

Fitzgerald (2013) Black bile: Are elevated monoamines an etiological factor in some cases of major depression? Med Hypotheses 80:823-6.

(Williams et al. 2003): "Published data from studies on the genetics of the serotonin reuptake "pump" may indeed suggest that few people are high in serotonin, although this is an area of active research."

Williams et al. (2003) Serotonin-related gene polymorphisms and central nervous system serotonin function. Neuropsychopharmacology 28:533-41.

Frederick K. Goodwin, Kay R. Jamison, *Manic-depressive Illness*, Oxford University Press, New York, NY, 1990.

Arnsten (2011) Catecholamine influences on dorsolateral prefrontal cortical networks. Biol Psychiatry 69:e89-99.

(Berman et al. 2000): "An exciting development in psychiatric drug treatment that has occurred in the last decade or so is the discovery that the "dissociative" (that is, reality distorting) anesthetic and drug of abuse, ketamine, has quickly-acting antidepressant properties in depressed persons."

Berman et al. (2000) Antidepressant effects of ketamine in depressed patients. Biol Psychiatry 47:351-4.

(Wachtel 1983): "One intriguing drug, which ties in with our earlier discussion of the signaling molecule cAMP, is called rolipram."

Wachtel (1983) Potential antidepressant activity of rolipram and other selective cyclic adenosine 3',5'-monophosphate phosphodiesterase inhibitors. Neuropharmacology 22:267-72.

(Suhonen et al. 1996): "Until the 1990s, it was widely believed that adult humans are not able to generate new neurons. Through the efforts of eminent neuroscientist Fred Gage at the Salk Institute in California and other scientists, this idea has since been shown incorrect."

Suhonen et al. (1996) Differentiation of adult hippocampus-derived progenitors into olfactory neurons in vivo. Nature 383:624-7.

(Santarelli et al. 2003): "Pioneering neuroscientist Rene Hen at Columbia University in New York, as well as other scientists, have shown that antidepressant drugs may boost mood in part by stimulating growth of new neurons in the hippocampus, a structure that connects with other brain circuits that may also contribute to mood and other depression-related characteristics."

Santarelli et al. (2003) Requirement of hippocampal neurogenesis for the behavioral effects of antidepressants. Science 301:805-9.

(Raichle et al. 2001): "Another aspect of brain function that has garnered increasing interest in recent years is the so-called default mode network. This term refers to a group of functionally intertwined brain regions that tend to be most active when we are daydreaming or "spacing out"."

Raichle et al. (2001) A default mode of brain function. Proc Natl Acad Sci USA 98:676-82.

(Izquierdo et al. 2006): "Neuroscientists such as Andrew Holmes at the National Institutes of Health in the United States have shown that exposing animals even to a single, brief stressor can alter the anatomical structures of neurons in the prefrontal cortex and elsewhere in the brain."

Izquierdo et al. (2006) Brief uncontrollable stress causes dendritic retraction in infralimbic cortex and resistance to fear extinction in mice. J Neurosci 26:5733-8.

Peter D. Kramer, *Against Depression*, Viking Penguin, New York, NY, 2005.

(Mayberg et al. 2005): "Another pioneer in the field of neuroscience is Helen Mayberg of Emory University in Atlanta. She has been at the forefront of using a technique called deep brain stimulation to treat persons with intractable cases of major depression."

Mayberg et al. (2005) Deep brain stimulation for treatment-resistant depression. Neuron 45:651-60.

CHAPTER 5. BETTER THAN WELL IN ACTION

(Logue et al. 1985): "For example, there is a drug called DSP-4 that can destroy a portion of norepinephrine neurons when given to animals."

Logue et al. (1985) Differential effects of DSP-4 administration on regional brain norepinephrine turnover in rats. Life Sci 37:403-9.

Marcia Angell, *The Truth About the Drug Companies*, Random House, New York, NY, 2005.

Irving Kirsch, *The Emperor's New Drugs*, Basic Books, New York, NY, 2011.

(Smoller et al. 2013): "Various psychiatric disorders may also share genetic underpinnings."

Smoller et al. (2013) Identification of risk loci with shared effects on five major psychiatric disorders: a genome-wide analysis. Lancet 381:1371-9.

CHAPTER 6. DEPRESSION AND BIPOLAR DISORDER

(Rapoport et al. 1980): "For example, attention deficit hyperactivity disorder (ADHD) appears to exist as a range in the population of children, based on direct measures of hyperactivity."

Rapoport et al. (1980) Dextroamphetamine. Its cognitive and behavioral effects in normal and hyperactive boys and normal men. Arch Gen Psychiatry 37:933-43.

(Uher et al. 2011): "A related point, described in *Listening to Prozac*, is that tricyclic antidepressants or norepinephrine boosting drugs in general may be more effective than SSRIs for treating severe depression, also known as melancholic depression. This remains an open and understudied question, and in my opinion some cases of severe depression may respond better to SSRIs than to norepinephrine boosting drugs."

Uher et al. (2011) Melancholic, atypical and anxious depression subtypes and outcome of treatment with escitalopram and nortriptyline. J Affect Disord 132:112-20.

(Fitzgerald 2013): "In a theoretical scientific paper published in 2013, I suggested that atypical depression is caused, at least in part, by elevated norepinephrine signaling."

Fitzgerald (2013) Black bile: Are elevated monoamines an etiological factor in some cases of major depression? Med Hypotheses 80:823-6.

(Joyce et al. 2004): "Consistent with this theory, a fairly recent study of atypical depression found that this disorder responds better to a serotonin boosting antidepressant than it does to a norepinephrine boosting one."

Joyce et al. (2004) Atypical depression, atypical temperament and a differential antidepressant response to fluoxetine and nortriptyline. Depress Anxiety 19:180-6.

(Williams et al. 2003): "One reason for thinking so involves a gene that regulates the expression of the serotonin reuptake transporter in the brain. The variants of this gene in the human population suggest that more people have high expression of the transporter, which would probably produce low levels of synaptic serotonin."

Williams et al. (2003) Serotonin-related gene polymorphisms and central nervous system serotonin function. Neuropsychopharmacology 28:533-41.

(For example, Harmer et al. 2004): "Catherine Harmer, Philip Cowen, and colleagues at Oxford University in England have performed a series of pioneering studies using antidepressants and related drugs that act on serotonin or norepinephrine, which indicate that these drugs bias emotional processing in humans so as to produce, in some ways at least, a more favorable or positive outlook."

Harmer et al. (2004) Increased positive versus negative affective perception and memory in healthy volunteers following selective serotonin and norepinephrine reuptake inhibition. Am J Psychiatry 161:1256-63.

(Fava et al. 2003): "A few years ago, a large study called Sequenced Treatment Alternatives to Relieve Depression (STAR*D, for short) was carried to out to assess the value of switching drugs when the first one does not work or only produces a weak response."

Fava et al. (2003) Background and rationale for the sequenced treatment alternatives to relieve depression (STAR*D) study. Psychiatr Clin North Am 26:457-94.

Kay R. Jamison, *Touched with Fire*, Free Press, New York, NY, 1993.

(Jimerson et al. 1981): "I also view bipolar disorder as being a largely genetic disease, which is characterized by elevated norepinephrine signaling in most persons who have it."

Jimerson et al. (1981) Plasma MHPG in rapid cyclers and healthy twins. Arch Gen Psychiatry 38:1287-90.

(For example, Alary and Andersson 1988): "One idea, which may be applicable to other mental illnesses as well, is that reducing norepinephrine signaling with existing pharmaceutical drugs may help treat many cases of unipolar depression, as well as bipolar disorder. While this is not a widely known treatment strategy for either disorder, there are a number of published scientific studies that support this approach."

Alary and Andersson (1988) Clonidine: prophylactic action in rapid cycling manic-depressive psychosis. Encephale 14:119-126.

(Fitzgerald 2013): "There are theoretical and empirical reasons for believing that drugs which act on monoamines may take a number of *years* to reach maximum effect."

Fitzgerald (2013) Forbearance for fluoxetine: Do monoaminergic antidepressants require a number of years to reach maximum therapeutic effect in humans? Int J Neurosci [Epub ahead of print].

CHAPTER 7. SCHIZOPHRENIA

(Horn and Snyder 1971, Carlsson 1977, Grace 1991): "Many variations of this "dopamine hypothesis" have been proposed since then, by such researchers as Solomon Snyder at Johns Hopkins University, Anthony Grace at the University of Pittsburgh and Nobel Prize laureate Arvid Carlsson of the University of Gothenburg in Sweden."

Grace AA (1991) Phasic versus tonic dopamine release and the modulation of dopamine system responsivity: a hypothesis for the etiology of schizophrenia. Neuroscience 41:1-24.

Carlsson A (1977) Does dopamine play a role in schizophrenia. Psychol Med 7:583-97.

Horn and Snyder (1971) Chlorpromazine and dopamine: conformational similarities that correlate with the antischizophrenic activity of phenothiazine drugs. Proc Natl Acad Sci USA 68:2325-8.

(Egan et al. 1998): "It is now widely believed that LSD and related hallucinogens achieve their psychedelic effects by activating the serotonin 5-HT$_{2A}$ receptor (although they may also interact with 5-HT$_{2C}$), consistent with the 5-HT$_{2A}$ receptor in particular and serotonin in general playing a role in schizophrenia."

Egan et al. (1998) Agonist activity of LSD and lisuride at cloned 5HT2A and 5HT2C receptors. Psychopharmacology (Berl) 136:409-14.

(Olney and Farber 1995): "The so-called "NMDA receptor hypofunction hypothesis of schizophrenia" suggests that underfunctioning of this important receptor subtype results in the disease."

Olney and Farber (1995) Glutamate receptor dysfunction and schizophrenia. Arch Gen Psychiatry 52:998-1007.

(Yamamoto et al. 1994, Yamamoto and Hornykiewicz 2004, Lechin and van der Dijs 2005): "A lesser known theory of schizophrenia suggests that elevated norepinephrine signaling is a cause of the disorder, particularly in the paranoid subtype of the illness."

Yamamoto et al. (1994) Possible noradrenergic dysfunction in schizophrenia. Brain Res Bull 35:529-43.

Yamamoto and Hornykiewicz (2004) Proposal for a noradrenaline hypothesis of schizophrenia. Prog Neuropsychopharmacol and Biol Psychiatry 28: 913-22.

Lechin and van der Dijs (2005) Noradrenergic hypothesis of schizophrenia. Prog Neuropsychopharmacol and Biol Psychiatry 29:777-8.

(Brixey et al. 1993): "The idea that norepinephrine is a factor in schizophrenia may tie in with the observation that when pregnant mothers are exposed to significant stress, their children are more likely to develop the disease later in life."

Brixey et al. (1993) Gestational and neonatal factors in the etiology of schizophrenia. J Clin Psychol 49:447-56.

(Fitzgerald 2012): "On the other hand, the overall effect of glutamate in the brain is excitatory, although in a 2012 paper I suggested that the effect of the NMDA receptor is largely inhibitory."

Fitzgerald (2012) The NMDA receptor may participate in widespread suppression of circuit level neural activity, in addition to a similarly prominent role in circuit level activation. Behav Brain Res 230:291-8.

(For example, Freedman et al. 1982): "There is evidence from human schizophrenia studies that at least some of these drugs have therapeutic efficacy in the disease, which may be comparable with standard antipsychotic drugs."

Freedman et al. (1982) Clonidine treatment of schizophrenia. Double-blind comparison to placebo and neuroleptic drugs. Acta Psychiatr Scand 65:35-45.

(Chang et al. 1990): "There is also some evidence that antipsychotic drugs may at least partially achieve their effects by lowering norepinephrine signaling."

Chang et al. (1990) Plasma catecholamine metabolites in schizophrenics: evidence for the two-subtype concept. Biol Psychiatr 27:510-18.

(Gaertner et al. 2002): "A related point is that tricyclic antidepressants, many of which *boost* norepinephrine signaling, can increase suicidality in persons with schizophrenia, making it questionable as to whether tricyclics should ever be used in the disorder."

Gaertner et al. (2002) A case control study on psychopharmacotherapy before suicide committed by 61 psychiatric inpatients. Pharmacopsychiatry 35:37-43.

(Thakore et al. 1996): "As stated earlier, acetylcholine may be very similar to serotonin in brain function, where both are essentially inhibitory neurotransmitters, so boosting serotonin with SSRI drugs may also be effective in schizophrenia."

Thakore et al. (1996) An open trial of adjunctive sertraline in the treatment of chronic schizophrenia. Acta Psychiatr Scand 94:194-7.

Chapter 8. Autism

(Kolevzon et al. 2006): "Perhaps the most well studied pharmaceutical treatment for autism, both in children and adults, is use of SSRIs, which may produce mild improvement in symptoms (although their efficacy has been questioned) in the manner in which these drugs are typically used."

Kolevzon et al. (2006) Selective serotonin reuptake inhibitors in autism: a review of efficacy and tolerability. J Clin Psychiatry 67:407-14.

(Grezes et al. 2003): "A number of brain regions, many of which may interact with prefrontal cortex, are home to an intriguing set of cells called "mirror neurons", which may be present both in humans and in animals."

Grezes et al. (2003) Activations related to "mirror" and "canonical" neurones in the human brain: an fMRI study. Neuroimage 18:928-37.

(Bari and Robbins 2013, Arnsten 2011): "Trevor Robbins of the University of Cambridge and Amy Arnsten of Yale University, pioneering researchers in studies of prefrontal cortex, have shown that serotonin, norepinephrine, and related molecules—as well as drugs that act on these systems—can dramatically affect the functional properties of prefrontal cortex."

Bari and Robbins (2013) Inhibition and impulsivity: behavioral and neural basis of response control. Prog Neurobiol 108:44-79.

Arnsten (2011) Catecholamine influences on dorsolateral prefrontal cortical networks. Biol Psychiatry 69:e89-99.

(Fitzgerald 2011): "In 2011, I published a theoretical paper on this topic, suggesting that serotonin plays a general role in activating prefrontal cortex, whereas norepinephrine deactivates this brain region."

Fitzgerald (2011) A neurochemical yin and yang: Does serotonin activate and norepinephrine deactivate the prefrontal cortex? Psychopharmacol (Berl) 213:171-82.

(Chez et al. 2004): "The second point relates to boosting serotonin with SSRIs and/or acetylcholine through cholinesterase inhibitors."

Chez et al. (2004) Treating autistic spectrum disorders in children: utility of the cholinesterase inhibitor rivastigmine tartrate. J Child Neurol 19:165-9.

Chapter 9. OCD

Lauren Slater, *Prozac Diary*, Random House, New York, NY, 1998.

(Fitzgerald 2011): "In a theoretical paper that I published in 2011, I suggested that serotonin may play a general role in activating prefrontal cortex, whereas norepinephrine tends to deactivate this brain region."

Fitzgerald (2011) A neurochemical yin and yang: Does serotonin activate and norepinephrine deactivate the prefrontal cortex? Psychopharmacol (Berl) 213:171-82.

(Baxter et al. 1987, Swedo et al. 1992): "OCD may principally result from overactive habitual circuitry in the brain, especially in terms of the basal ganglia, although an overactive orbitofrontal cortex may also play a role, according to brain imaging studies in humans."

Baxter et al. (1987) Local cerebral glucose metabolic rates in obsessive-compulsive disorder. A comparison with rates in unipolar depression and in normal controls. Arch Gen Psychiatry 44:211-8.

Swedo et al. (1992) Cerebral glucose metabolism in childhood-onset obsessive-compulsive disorder. Revisualization during pharmacotherapy. Arch Gen Psychiatry 49:690-4.

(Fineberg et al. 2013): "Conventional drug treatment for OCD tends to employ SSRIs such as Prozac (or the serotonin boosting drug, clomipramine), often given at high doses."

Fineberg et al. (2013) Pharmacotherapy of obsessive-compulsive disorder: evidence-based treatment and beyond. Aust N Z J Psychiatry 47:121-41.

CHAPTER 10. DRUG AND ALCOHOL ABUSE

(Weinshenker and Schroeder 2007): "David Weinshenker at Emory University has been carrying out pioneering work in norepinephrine for a number of years, including implicating this transmitter in reward."

Weinshenker and Schroeder (2007) There and back again: a tale of norepinephrine and drug addiction. Neuropsychopharmacology 32:1433-51.

(Cloninger 1986): "The ideas of the eminent psychiatric researcher, C. Robert Cloninger, particularly implicate dopamine in stimulus or novelty seeking."

Cloninger (1986) A unified biosocial theory of personality and its role in the development of anxiety states. Psychiatr Dev 4:167-226.

(Fitzgerald 2013): "An idea that I have been developing in recent years is that elevated norepinephrine signaling—whether as a result of genetics, exposure to significant stress, or both—is a shared, major factor in a wide range of substance abuse disorders."

Fitzgerald (2013) Elevated Norepinephrine may be a Unifying Etiological Factor in the Abuse of a Broad Range of Substances: Alcohol, Nicotine, Marijuana, Heroin, Cocaine, and Caffeine. Subst Abuse 7:171-83.

(Fitzgerald 2012): "In a 2012 paper, I reviewed some of these data, which suggest among other things that alcohol intake is intimately related with the very production of norepinephrine by the body's own biochemical pathways."

Fitzgerald PJ (2012) Neurodrinking: is alcohol a substrate in a novel, endogenous synthetic pathway for norepinephrine? Med Hypotheses 78:760-2.

(Van Bockstaele et al. 2008, Manvich et al. 2013): "An intriguing point is that two drugs, naltrexone and Antabuse, that are commonly used to reduce alcohol intake in humans, may partly achieve their therapeutic effects by acting on norepinephrine signaling."

Van Bockstaele et al. (2008) Low dose naltrexone administration in morphine dependent rats attenuates withdrawal-induced norepinephrine efflux in forebrain. Prog Neuropsychopharmacol Biol Psychiatry 32:1048-56.

Manvich et al. (2013) Dopamine β-Hydroxylase Inhibitors Enhance the Discriminative Stimulus Effects of Cocaine in Rats. J Pharmacol Exp Ther [Epub ahead of print].

CHAPTER 11. ADHD, RITALIN, AND COGNITIVE ENHANCEMENT

Daniel G. Amen, *Healing ADD*, Putnam, New York, NY, 2001.

(Constantinidis et al. 2001, Katsuki and Constantinidis 2012): "The work of neuroscientists such as Christos Constantinidis at Wake Forest University, and the late Patricia Goldman-Rakic from Yale University, suggests that the posterior parietal cortex and prefrontal cortex work together to allow us to focus on things, while also affecting our ability to form short-term memories."

Constantinidis et al. (2001) The sensory nature of mnemonic representation in the primate prefrontal cortex. Nat Neurosci 4:311-6.

Katsuki and Constantinidis (2012) Unique and shared roles of the posterior parietal and dorsolateral prefrontal cortex in cognitive functions. Front Integr Neurosci 6:17.

(Cole et al. 2012): "A recent study has suggested that intelligence itself may be related to how well disparate regions of the brain work together: a neural connectedness theory."

Cole et al. (2012) Global connectivity of prefrontal cortex predicts cognitive control and intelligence. J Neurosci 32:8988-99.

(Bymaster et al. 2002): "Strattera, a drug that in recent years was added to the repertoire of treatments for ADHD, may primarily work by boosting brain norepinephrine, although there is some evidence that it also boosts prefrontal dopamine."

Bymaster et al. (2002) Atomoxetine increases extracellular level of norepinephrine and dopamine in prefrontal cortex of rat: a potential mechanism for efficacy in attention deficit/hyperactivity disorder. Neuropsychopharmacology 27:699-711.

(Arnsten and Pliszka 2011, Del Campo et al. 2011): "The ideas of two pioneering researchers mentioned earlier, Amy Arnsten and Trevor Robbins, strongly implicate norepinephrine and dopamine (and possibly other transmitters) in our ability, and that of animals, to pay attention to things that are of interest."

Arnsten and Pliszka (2011) Catecholamine influences on prefrontal cortical function: relevance to treatment of attention deficit/hyperactivity disorder and related disorders. Pharmacol Biochem Behav 99:211-6.

Del Campo et al. (2011) The roles of dopamine and noradrenaline in the pathophysiology and treatment of attention-deficit/hyperactivity disorder. Biol Psychiatry 69:e145-57.

(Fitzgerald 2011, 2012): "My reasoning is that there is evidence that lowering norepinephrine may increase activation of the prefrontal cortex, also activation of much of the right brain hemisphere, and perhaps particularly the right prefrontal cortex."

Fitzgerald (2011) A neurochemical yin and yang: Does serotonin activate and norepinephrine deactivate the prefrontal cortex? Psychopharmacol (Berl) 213:171-82.

Fitzgerald (2012) Whose side are you on: does serotonin preferentially activate the right hemisphere and norepinephrine the left? Med Hypotheses 79:250-4.

Chapter 12. PTSD, trauma, and stress

James Gleick, *Chaos*, Viking, New York, NY, 1987.

James Gleick, *Faster*, Little, Brown & Company, New York, NY, 1999.

(For example, Rodriguez-Romaguera et al. 2009, Karpova et al. 2011): "The existing data suggest that drugs which act on serotonin or norepinephrine, for example, can modulate the ability of mice and rats to extinguish their fear."

Rodriguez-Romaguera et al. (2009) Systemic propranolol acts centrally to reduce conditioned fear in rats without impairing extinction. Biol Psychiatr 65:887-92.

Karpova et al. (2011) Fear erasure in mice requires synergy between antidepressant drugs and extinction training. Science 334:1731-4.

(Krystal and Neumeister 2009): "Not surprisingly, the neurotransmitter norepinephrine is already perhaps the signaling molecule most directly implicated in PTSD, partly because it is released in the brain and the rest of the body in response to psychological stress. Serotonin has also received a lot of attention with regard to PTSD."

Krystal and Neumeister (2009) Noradrenergic and serotonergic mechanisms in the neurobiology of posttraumatic stress disorder and resilience. Brain Res 1293:13-23.

CHAPTER 13. THE "WORRIED WELL", NEUROTICISM, AND EXPANDED DYSTHYMIA

Gary Marcus, *Kluge*, Houghton Mifflin, New York, NY, 2008.

David J. Linden, *The Accidental Mind*, Harvard University Press, Cambridge, MA, 2007.

Michael J. Norden, *Beyond Prozac*, ReganBooks, New York, NY, 1995.

Paul J. Fitzgerald, *Adjust Your Brain*, O Books, Winchester, United Kingdom, 2007.

Stephen Braun, *The Science of Happiness*, Wiley, Hoboken, NJ, 2000.

John J. Ratey, Catherine Johnson, *Shadow Syndromes*, Bantam Books, New York, NY, 1998.

Antonio R. Damasio, *Descartes' Error*, Picador, New York, NY, 1994.

(Papousek et al. 2013): "On the other hand, serotonin (the molecule that Prozac boosts) has been associated with production of negative emotion in some scientific studies."

Papousek et al. (2013) Serotonin Transporter Genotype (5-HTTLPR) and Electrocortical Responses Indicating the Sensitivity to Negative Emotional Cues. Emotion [Epub ahead of print].

CHAPTER 14. BETTER THAN WELL FOR THE BODY

(Fitzgerald 2009a,b; 2010a,b,c; 2012; 2013a,b,c): "In my own published work, I have suggested that the extracellular (that is, outside of cells) signaling molecule and neurotransmitter, norepinephrine, plays a very prominent role in many of the major diseases of the body, and possibly in many of the less common ones too."

Fitzgerald PJ (2009a) Is elevated noradrenaline an aetiological factor in a number of diseases? Auton Autacoid Pharmacol 29:143-56.

Fitzgerald PJ (2009b) Is norepinephrine an etiological factor in some types of cancer? Int J Cancer 124:257-63.

Fitzgerald PJ (2010a) Is elevated norepinephrine an etiological factor in some cases of Alzheimer's disease? Curr Alzheimer Res 7:506-16.

Fitzgerald PJ (2010b) Is elevated norepinephrine an etiological factor in some cases of epilepsy? Seizure 19:311-8.

Fitzgerald PJ (2010c) Testing whether drugs that weaken norepinephrine signaling prevent or treat various types of cancer. Clin Epidemiol 2:1-3.

Fitzgerald PJ (2012) Beta blockers, norepinephrine, and cancer: an epidemiological viewpoint. Clin Epidemiol 4:151-6.

Fitzgerald PJ (2013a) Black bile: Are elevated monoamines an etiological factor in some cases of major depression? Med Hypotheses 80:823-6.

Fitzgerald PJ (2013b) Elevated norepinephrine may be an etiological factor in a wide range of diseases: age-related macular degeneration, systemic lupus erythematosus, atrial fibrillation, metabolic syndrome. Med Hypotheses 80:558-63.

Fitzgerald PJ (2013c) Elevated Norepinephrine May Be a Unifying Etiological Factor in the Abuse of a Broad Range of Substances: Alcohol, Nicotine, Marijuana, Heroin, Cocaine, and Caffeine. Substance Abuse: Research and Treatment 7:171-83.

Carl Elliot, *Better than Well: American Medicine Meets the American Dream*, W. W. Norton & Company, New York, NY, 2003.

CHAPTER 15. SOCIOPATHY, PSYCHOTICISM, AND CREATIVITY

(Eysenck and Eysenck 1977): "Hans Eysenck, the late and highly accomplished psychologist, helped put forth a controversial personality model decades ago that was based in three elements: psychoticism, extraversion, and neuroticism (P-E-N, for short), suggesting that variation in these characteristics may largely explain the diversity of human behavior."

(Eysenck and Eysenck 1977) The place of impulsiveness in a dimensional system of personality description. Br J Soc Clin Psychol 16:57-68.

Martha Stout, *The Sociopath Next Door*, Broadway Books, New York, NY, 2005.

M. E. Thomas, *Confessions of a Sociopath*, Crown, New York, NY, 2013.

(Burch et al. 2006): "On the other hand, schizotypy, which may be a milder variant of full-blown schizophrenia, is associated with above average levels of creativity."

Burch et al. (2006) Schizotypy and creativity in visual artists. Br J Psychol 97:177-90.

(Kyaga et al. 2011): "Also, unaffected family members of persons with these mental disorders exhibit above average levels of creativity."

Kyaga et al. (2011) Creativity and mental disorder: family study of 300,000 people with severe mental disorder. Br J Psychiatry 199:373-9.

Kay R. Jamison, *Touched with Fire*, Free Press, New York, NY, 1993.

(Dzirasa et al. 2006): "Duke University neuroscientist Miguel Nicolelis and co-workers have suggested that elevated dopaminergic signaling may produce a superimposition of the sleeping mind on the waking one (to frame this in Freudian terms, as they did in one of their publications)."

Dzirasa et al. (2006) Dopaminergic control of sleep-wake states. J Neurosci 26:10577-89.

CHAPTER 16. DOMINANCE AND EMINENCE

(Tse and Bond 2002): "One of the scientific studies I referred to earlier suggested that a serotonin boosting antidepressant can modulate assertiveness and even degree of eye contact among people sharing an apartment."

Tse and Bond (2002) Serotonergic intervention affects both social dominance and affiliative behaviour. Psychopharmacology (Berl) 161:324-30.

(For example, Raleigh 1987): "This nearly humorous observation suggests that serotonin plays a role in social dominance, a view that has indeed been supported by a number of human and animal studies, many of which assert that boosting serotonin increases social dominance. However, conflicting findings have been reported."

Raleigh (1987) Differential behavioral effects of tryptophan and 5-hydroxytryptophan in vervet monkeys: influence of catecholaminergic systems. Psychopharmacology (Berl) 93:44-50.

John D. Gartner, *The Hypomanic Edge*, Simon & Schuster, New York, NY, 2005.

Paul J. Fitzgerald, Ph.D.

Arnold M. Ludwig, *The Price of Greatness*, The Guilford Press, New York, NY, 1995.

Samuel H. Barondes, *Mood Genes*, W.H. Freeman & Company, New York, NY, 1998.

CHAPTER 18. MORALITY AND ETHICS

Peter R. Breggin, *Toxic Psychiatry*, St. Martin's Press, New York, NY, 1991.

Peter R. Breggin and David Cohen, *Your Drug May Be Your Problem*, Da Capo Press, New York, NY, 1999.

Aldous Huxley, *Brave New World*, Harper & Brothers, New York, NY, 1932.

(Crockett et al. 2010): "A recent scientific paper, mentioned in Chapter 2, suggests that boosting serotonin with antidepressants such as SSRIs may enhance moral decision making."

Crockett et al. (2010) Serotonin selectively influences moral judgment and behavior through effects on harm aversion. Proc Natl Acad Sci USA 107:17433-8.

CHAPTER 19. FUTURISM, SOCIETY, AND GENERAL CONCLUSIONS

Ray Kurzweil, *The Age of Spiritual Machines*, Viking, New York, NY, 1999.

Ray Kurzweil, *The Singularity is Near*, Viking, New York, NY, 2005.

(Samuel H. Barondes 2003): "But, as Samuel Barondes points out, perhaps drugs with similar mechanisms of action to these could be produced that don't cause sedation as a side effect."

Samuel H. Barondes, *Better than Prozac*, Oxford University Press, New York, NY, 2003.